# The *Stretch&Sew* Sewing Book
## Part 2

# The Stretch & Sew Sewing Book Part 2

## By Ann Person

Published by Stretch & Sew, Inc.
Eugene, Oregon

# Contents

# Introduction

At one time in my life I was told that to be really successful you should find a job you could be paid to do and yet would gladly do for nothing. And it's true. If you enjoy your job, it no longer seems like work.

Teaching new ways to sew with knits was that kind of a job for me. I knew it when I taught my first class. And I knew it in the excitement of designing and selling my first pattern. But never in those early days did I imagine that my first Stretch & Sew® classes would grow to become a company of the size and importance of the Stretch & Sew we know today.

Yes, with that growth my work has changed. My job is not the same as it was in the beginning. Still, the love of the work and the thrill of being part of a company that has been responsible for developing so many new and wonderful sewing techniques is as great now as it was in my first class so many years ago.

The success of our first *Stretch & Sew®* sewing book, published in 1967, was a milestone in my career. Countless thousands of women and men have learned to sew with knits using the Stretch & Sew book as their guide. All with the help of the many, many wonderful Stretch & Sew employees, franchise store owners and the now more than 2,000 licensed Stretch & Sew teachers who have trained at our headquarters in Eugene.

Over the years, these members of the Stretch & Sew family have also contributed their own sewing skills and creativity to our success story. Their ideas are incorporated in this new sewing book.

*Stretch & Sew Sewing Book, Part 2* is full of new sewing information. Yet the basic concept from which Stretch & Sew has grown is still here. The premise that sewing should be uncomplicated to be truly enjoyable and rewarding. Simple, yes, but simplicity without sacrificing style. Using Stretch & Sew techniques, you learn to sew garments with quality and appearance that avoid any "homemade" connotation. And you have fun with your sewing projects. After all, why would anyone spend time to make stylish clothes if it wasn't fun? As we develop still newer Stretch & Sew ideas, we won't lose sight of the fundamentals. Keep it simple and keep it fun.

Our goal here, with *Stretch & Sew Sewing Book, Part 2,* is to stimulate your creativity. To give you additional skills with which to work. To take you beyond the Stretch & Sew basics you already know and enhance your creative sewing abilities even more.

Many of you also know that the Stretch & Sew® Patterns you'll be using with this book are designed to be interchangeable, giving you more opportunity for personal creativity. For instance, a dress sleeve from a Stretch & Sew Pattern can also serve as a sleeve of a blouse. The collar from the shell pattern will work on dress necklines. Garments of similar design are interchangeable to give you greater versatility and, of course, a free rein on creativity.

Now, with the knowledge of flat pattern techniques found here, you can not only interchange sleeves but you actually will be able to redesign the basic dress. Ideas and techniques that never before have been offered to the home seamstress are here for you in this new book.

So have a good time. Experiment with ideas of your own. Sew garments that will give you satisfaction and pleasure. Not just in the wearing but also in the sewing.

Happy sewing.

Ann Person
Eugene, Oregon.

**1**

# Mitered V-Neck Knit Top with an Inset Cardigan Jacket with a Self-Trim Band

# Mitered V-Neck Knit Top with an Inset Cardigan Jacket with a Self-Trim Band

For years Stretch & Sew knit top patterns have been the basis for many variations in design. And the unique simplicity of these patterns lends itself easily to versatility in use of fabric as well.

The general principles found in Chapter One of *The Stretch & Sew Sewing Book* serve as a foundation for the first chapter in this series of exciting and new techniques. You will learn some of the things that can be done with knit top patterns which will enable you to be a creative designer in your own home.

## Patterns for These Techniques

*Set-In Sleeve Knit Top and Sweater Pattern 300* ✓
*Infants' Combination Pattern 850*
*Children's Set-In Sleeve Top Pattern 861*
*Set-In Sleeve Tab Front Shirt Pattern 1750* ✓

## General Fabric Selection

Your choice of fabrics for these garments is as varied as knits themselves. Fiber content is not a determining factor. The percent of stretch and the weight or bulk of the fabric are the principles that will dictate your selection. My old standby is the fabric's "hand." How does the fabric feel? Firm? Soft? Textured? Smooth? The choices are unlimited and, as always, the effect that you — the designer — want to achieve is the most important consideration.

Our knit top patterns were designed to fit most accurately with a fabric that has 25 percent stretch. If you select a fabric that does not have 25 percent stretch, you will have to adjust the size you use accordingly.

To determine the amount of stretch a fabric has, fold your fabric at least 10 inches from one cut edge. Take 10 inches of the fabric on the fold and stretch it. If your fabric will stretch easily to 12-1/2 inches, it has 25 percent stretch.

If the fabric will stretch to only 11-1/4 inches, it has 12-1/2 percent stretch and it will be necessary for you to cut your knit top one size larger. If the 10 inches of fabric stretches to 15 inches, the fabric has 50 percent stretch. In this case, you will have a better fit if you cut the knit top one size smaller. (Fig. 1) The important thing to remember is that the stretch in your fabric becomes ease in your garment.

The fabrics most often used for the mitered V-neck top with an inset are single and double knit cottons and single and double knit polyesters. If you have selected two fabric weights, you should use the heavier fabric for the main part of the garment. The lighter weight fabric will adapt nicely for the inset, emphasizing the layered effect. A rib knit trim is necessary for finishing the neck unless you apply a zipper.

The contrast in fabrics that you choose will add interest to your garment. You may coordinate striped or print fabric with a solid fabric in a

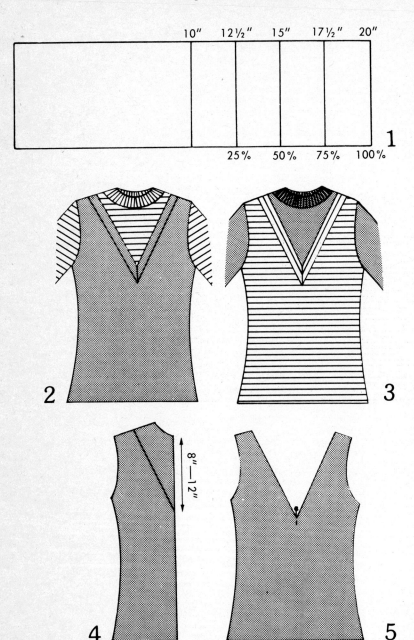

variety of ways. For example, the solid color may be used for the V-neck trim and the main part of the garment with the stripe or print used for the inset and sleeves. Pick up the solid color again with the rib knit neck trim. (Fig. 2) Reverse this combination and you have created a new effect. (Fig. 3)

## Mitered V-Neck Knit Top with an Inset

## Cutting and Sewing Your Garment

You will need to cut one back, one front, and two sleeves from your pattern. An additional piece of fabric, approximately 10 inches by 12 to 15 inches, will be required for the inset.

Fold the front of the knit top exactly in half to cut the V. Measure down the center front fold 8 to 12 inches, depending on the depth of the V you would like. Cut from this point to the middle of the shoulder edges. Cutting in the opposite direction might cause an uneven point in your V. (Fig. 4) Save the piece cut from the front because it will be used later as a pattern for the inset.

Cut two strips of trim for the mitered V finish with the greater stretch going the length of the strip. These strips should be self-trim. In other words, they should be cut from the same fabric as you use in the main part of the garment. Each strip should measure 2-1/2 inches wide by the length of one side of the V plus about 1-1/2 inches. Fold each strip in half lengthwise, wrong sides together, and press, taking care not to stretch them.

Position a pin straight down from the point of the V to establish the exact place where you must start and stop your stitching. The head of the pin should be above the cut edge of the V so that it will not interfere with your sewing. (Fig. 5)

Position one folded strip of trim along the neck edge on the right side of the knit top. Make sure the cut edges are even and leave a 1-inch extension below the V. (Fig. 6) Using a 1/4-inch seam allowance and a 1:1 ratio — 1 inch of trim to 1 inch of garment neck edge — sew from the point of the V up to the shoulder. The stitching should start exactly at the pin. Slowly insert the needle into the fabric until it touches the pin.

Place the second strip of trim on the opposite neck edge of the knit top with the cut edges even. Start stitching with a 1/4-inch seam allowance from the shoulder seam to a point 1 inch from the center of the V. Fold the first strip back out of the way. Then, continue sewing the last inch until you reach the pin at the point of the V. There should be 1 inch of trim extending beyond the stitching. Hand-wheel the sewing machine the last few stitches so that the needle will not be damaged when it touches the pin. (Fig. 7)

For a good miter, it is very important that the two stitching lines meet exactly at the point of the V. It is easy to check the accuracy of your stitching by examining the wrong side of the garment. (Fig. 8) If adjustments are necessary, make them from the wrong side.

Clip to the point of the V, being careful not to cut into the stitching lines. (Fig. 9) Turn the trim into its finished position, tucking the tab extensions to the inside. Now, fold the front exactly in half with the right sides together.

The miter on the trim must be sewn in an exact line with the center front fold. You can be sure of this by marking your seamline for the miter on the trim with a ruler and a fine edge of soap. Or, you may pull the top thread from your sewing machine forward so that it is in line with

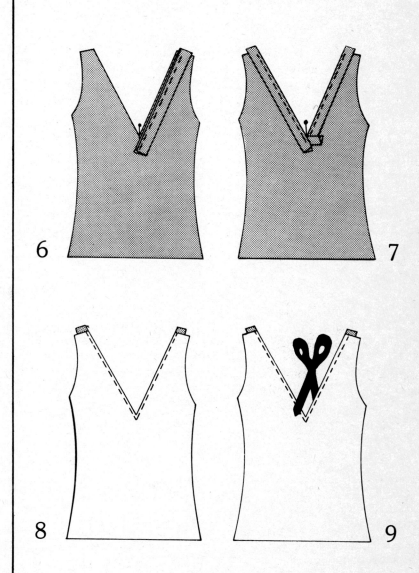

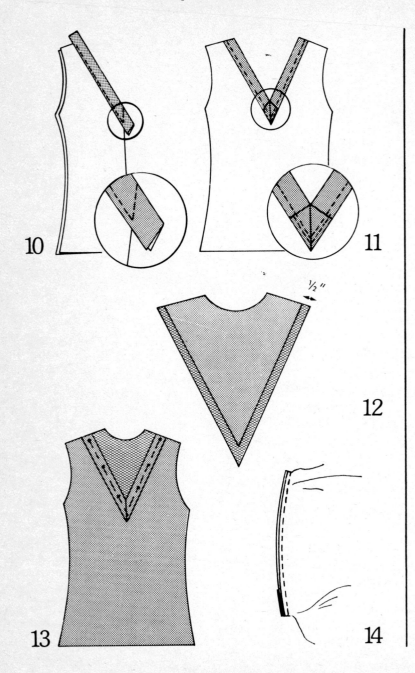

10

11

½ "

12

13

14

the center front fold as you sew. Since the locking of stitches is so critical when you sew the mitered V, start sewing about three stitches down from the folded edges of the trim. Backtack to the folds. Then, sew down to the point of the V and backtack again for about three stitches. (Fig. 10)

Fold each tab extension back and stitch it to the seam allowance. (Fig. 11) This will give a finished look to the inside of the garment and will also reinforce the V.

Position the V-shaped piece, that was cut from the front, on your fabric as a pattern for the inset. Make sure you have placed it on the straight-of-grain. Add a seam allowance of 1/2 inch to each side of the V, leaving the neck and shoulder edges the same. (Fig. 12)

Place the inset behind the mitered V and match the seam allowances exactly to those of the garment and the trim. Attach the inset to the front by pinning through the trim close to the folded edge. (Fig. 13) Fold back one side of the garment, exposing the seam allowance. Sew over the previous stitching line, including the inset in this stitching. (Fig. 14) On the other side, sew the inset in the same way.

The inset is now complete. You are back to where you began with a front, a back, and two sleeves, but with exciting new detail added in front.

The next step is to sew the shoulder seams. Press these seams to the back of the garment.

The neck trim is applied at this time. The amount to be cut away from the neck edge and the width and length of trim you will need depend upon the style you select. The ratios to determine the length of rib knit to cut for each neckline style follow. They are intended as general guidelines to be used with trim that has approximately 50 to 75 percent stretch.

If you are using trim with less stretch, cut it longer. Cut trim with greater stretch shorter. A good way to make sure you have the right length is to place the folded length of trim around the neck just as you want it to fit when finished, making sure it .will pull comfortably over the head. Mark the strip at this length after you have added 1/2 inch for seam allowance.

The crew neck, which follows the natural neckline, is a comfortable and attractive style. (Fig. 15) First, cut 3/4 inch from the entire neck edge. Cut rib trim that is 2-1/2 to 3 inches wide and as long as two-thirds the measurement of the neck edge seamline plus 1/2 inch for seam allowance.

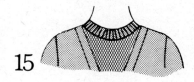

15

A mock turtleneck extends higher on the neck. (Fig. 16) For this style, cut 1/2 inch from the entire neck edge. Try the neck opening on and trim away another 1/8 inch if it does not fit comfortably over your head. A second 1/8 inch may be trimmed away if necessary. Cut rib trim that is 3 to 5 inches wide and three-quarters the length of the neck edge plus 1/2 inch for seam allowance.

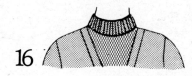

16

A turtleneck extends high on the neck and folds down to cover the seam at the natural neckline. (Fig. 17) If the opening fits comfortably over the head, do not trim it. Otherwise, trim away 1/8 inch and, if necessary, a second 1/8 inch. The rib trim should be cut 8 to 10 inches wide and as long as the neck edge plus 1/2 inch for seam allowance. This will give you a true turtleneck and the trim will fold down to cover

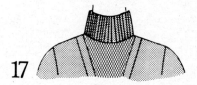

17

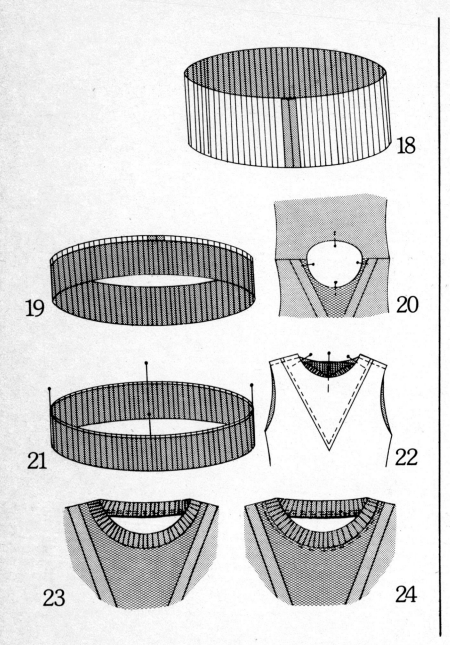

18

19

20

21

22

23

24

the neck seam. If you would prefer a snugger neck finish, cut your trim with a 3:4 ratio as you would for a mock turtleneck.

Whatever style you have selected, the procedure for applying the trim is the same. Open the rib knit trim out flat and, right sides together, sew the two ends with a 1/4-inch seam to form a cylinder. (Fig. 18) Finger-press the seam open and fold the trim in half lengthwise with wrong sides together. (Fig. 19) Divide both the neck edge of the garment (Fig. 20) and the cylinder of trim (Fig. 21) into fourths, marking each quarter point with a pin.

Pin the seam of the rib trim to the center back of the knit top with right sides together. Match all quarter divisions, pinning the trim to the neck edge at each point. (Fig. 22) Sew the rib trim to the neck edge, stretching the ribbing evenly to follow the neck opening. Press the seam allowance downward into the garment.

Three popular ways to finish the neck edge are as follows:

1. Sew a second row of straight stitching on the seam allowance 1/8 inch from the cut edge of the neckband. (Fig. 23)

2. Stretching slightly, topstitch around the entire neck edge 1/8 inch from the seamline into the garment. This will hold the seam allowance in place. (Fig. 24)

3. Sew a second row of straight stitching 1/8 inch from the cut edge of the neckband seam allowance on the front. Then, stretching slightly, topstitch, starting at the shoulder sleeve edge. Sew across one shoulder, across the back of the neck, and out to the other shoulder sleeve edge.

Catch the shoulder and the neck edge seam allowance in the stitching. (Fig. 25)

One of the basic differences between sewing with woven fabric and sewing on knit fabric is illustrated by the ease with which one may stretch a sleeve into a knit garment.

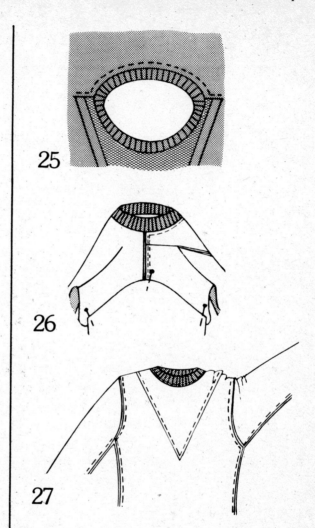

25

Divide the sleeve in half and mark this point. With right sides together, pin the sleeve to the knit top at the underarm and shoulder. Match the shoulder seam to the halfway point on the sleeve. (Fig. 26) With the sleeve next to your sewing machine, stitch the seam, stretching the armscye to fit the sleeve. For extra strength, sew another row of stitching 1/8 inch from the cut edge. Then, repeat these steps for the second sleeve.

26

Pin the front and back of the knit top together at the lower corners, at the underarm points, and at the sleeve edges with right sides together. Stretching as you sew, stitch the side seams from the lower edge of the garment, through the armscye, and out to the end of the sleeve seam. (Fig. 27) A second row of stitching 1/8 inch from the cut edges will give extra strength to the finished garment.

27

Finish the sleeves and lower edge by applying rib knit trim, by using *Perky Bond* fusible web, or by hemming with a machine stitch, and you will have completed your mitered V-neck knit top!

# Variations

### MITERED V-NECK TOP WITH RIB KNIT FOR TRIM ON THE V

When you are sewing the mitered V-neck top with an inset and want to trim it with rib knit, stretch the trim slightly from the point of the V to the shoulder seam. This is necessary because of the greater stretch of rib knit. The same is true for self-trim that is especially stretchy.

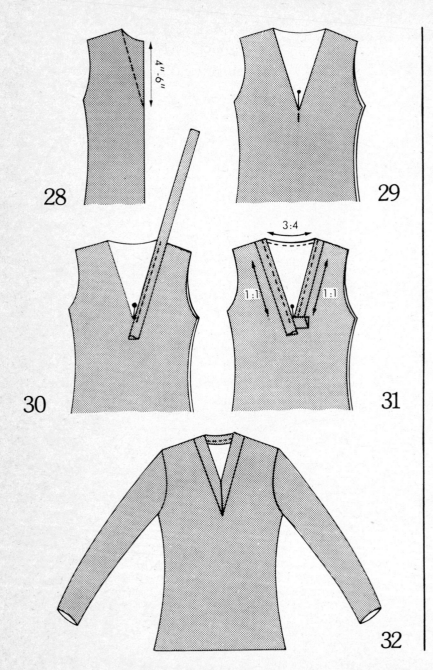

28

29

30

31

32

## MITERED V-NECK TOP WITHOUT AN INSET

Cut the garment with one back, one front, and two sleeves as you would for a regular knit top. If you prefer a neck finish that will fall from your natural neckline rather than from slightly above it, trim 3/4 to 1 inch from the total neck edge now. Fold the front in half lengthwise to cut the V. Measure down the center front fold 4 to 6 inches, depending on the depth of the V that you would like. (Fig. 28) Cut from this point on the center front fold to the shoulder neck edge. Then, sew the back to the front at the shoulder seams.

Cut one long strip of self-trim, 2-1/2 inches wide and the length of the total neck edge plus 2 to 3 inches. Fold the trim lengthwise, wrong sides together, and press lightly, taking care not to stretch it.

Position a pin at the point of the V to establish the exact place where you will start and stop your stitching. (Fig. 29) Put the trim on the right side of the garment with the cut edges of the trim even with the neck edge. Taking care to start exactly at the pin, stitch with a 1:1 ratio and a 1/4-inch seam allowance from the point of the V to the shoulder seam. (Fig. 30)

Continue stitching the trim to the back neck edge, stretching the trim with a 3:4 ratio — 3 inches of trim to 4 inches of garment neck edge — so that the trim will hug in closely to the neck. From the second shoulder seam back down to the point of the V, the stitching should be at a 1:1 ratio. (Fig. 31)

Miter and finish the V and complete the garment as previously described, omitting the inset. Your top will be fun to wear and so comfortable for any occasion! (Fig. 32)

## RIB KNIT TRIM ON MITERED V-NECK TOP WITHOUT AN INSET

Applying rib knit trim to this top is similar to the way you apply it to the top with an inset. Stretch the trim slightly as you sew it from the point of the V to the shoulder seam and stretch it with a 2:3 ratio as you sew it to the back neck edge. Continue sewing down to the point of the V, again stretching the trim slightly.

## MITERED SQUARE-NECK TOP WITH AN INSET

Fold the front in half to cut out the square. Measure down the center front fold 8 to 10 inches and connect that point to a line that is drawn straight down from the center of the shoulder. (Fig. 33) Cut the square away, saving it to use as a guide for the inset pattern.

Cut three strips of self-trim 2-1/2 inches wide. One strip should be the length of the lower edge of the square plus 2 inches. The other two should each be the length of the vertical side of the square plus 1-1/2 inches. Fold the strips in half lengthwise, wrong sides together, and press them lightly.

Place a pin at a 45 degree angle in each corner of the square. (Fig. 34) Position the first strip across the lower edge of the square on the right side of the front with the three cut edges together. One inch of trim should extend beyond each corner. Stitch with a 1:1 ratio and a 1/4-inch seam allowance from pin to pin, taking care to start and stop exactly at the pin as you did for the mitered V-neck. (Fig. 35)

Position a strip of trim on one side of the square with 1 inch extending beyond the corner. Fold the trim at the lower edge of the square out

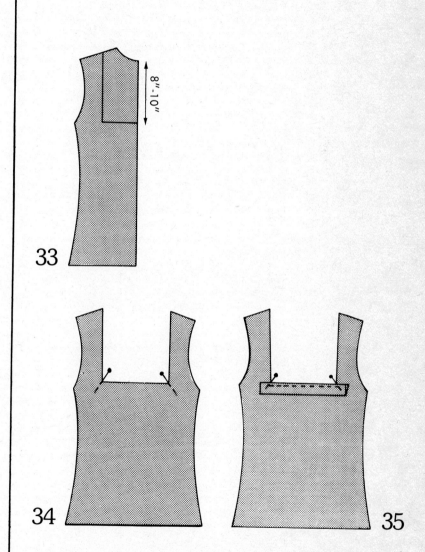

8"-10"

33

34

35

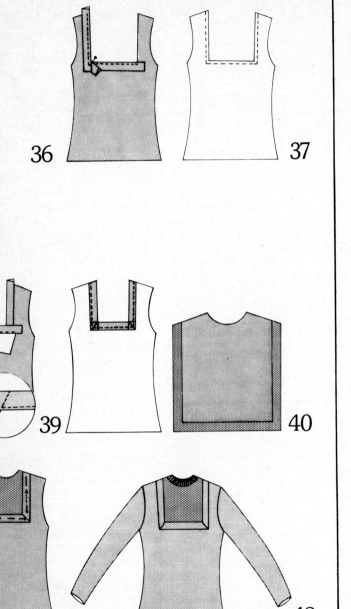

36

37

38    39

40

41    42

of the way and stitch from the pin to the shoulder. (Fig. 36) Do the same on the other side of the square. Check the wrong side of the front to be sure that the stitching lines meet exactly in the corners. This is a must for a good miter. (Fig. 37) Clip into the seam allowance at each corner, taking care not to cut through the stitching lines.

Turn the trim into position, tucking the tab extensions to the inside. Fold the front, right sides together, at one corner of the square. You may be sure your miter is at a 45 degree angle to the corner by placing the edge of the vertical trim against the edge of the horizontal trim. The fold that appears in the garment front will indicate the stitching line for the miter just as the center front foldline did for the mitered V-neck finish.

Sew the miter (Fig. 38) and complete it by folding back each tab end and stitching it to the seam allowance. Cut any excess trim even with the seam allowance. Repeat for the second corner of the square and press carefully. (Fig. 39)

Cut the inset piece, using the square that was cut from the front as a pattern, and add 1/2 inch for seam allowance to the cut edges of the square. Do not add to the neck and shoulder edges. (Fig. 40)

Position the inset piece on the wrong side of the front, matching the cut edges to the trim seam allowance. On the right side, pin along the folded edge of the trim to secure the inset. (Fig. 41) Turn up the lower edge of the front and, including the inset, sew over the previous stitching line. Fold back each side and do the same.

Complete the knit top, following the previous instructions. It will be a delight to wear and you created it yourself! (Fig. 42)

## MITERED SQUARE-NECK TOP
## WITH RIB KNIT FOR TRIM
## ON THE SQUARE

When you are sewing this top, stretch the rib trim slightly along all the edges of the square. Apply self-trim that is especially stretchy in the same way.

## MITERED SQUARE-NECK TOP
## WITHOUT AN INSET

If you would like the neck trim to fall from the natural neckline rather than from slightly above it, trim 3/4 to 1 inch away from the total neck edge before starting. Fold the front in half to cut the square. Measure down the center front fold 4 to 6 inches, depending on the depth that you prefer. Connect this point to a line drawn straight down from the shoulder neck edge. (Fig. 43) Starting at the folded edge, cut out the square.

Sew the shoulder seams together. Cut two strips of self-trim, 2-1/2 inches wide. One strip should measure the length of the lower edge of the square plus 2 inches. The other should measure the length of the neck from one corner of the square, around the back of the neck, and down to the other corner, plus 2 to 3 inches. This will be slightly more trim than is necessary. Lightly press the strips in half lengthwise, wrong sides together.

Place a pin in each corner at a 45 degree angle to guide you in starting and ending the stitching. (Fig. 44) Sew the shorter strip to the lower edge of the square with a 1/4-inch seam allowance and 1:1 ratio, leaving 1-inch extensions at the corners. Be careful to start and end your stitching exactly at the pins.

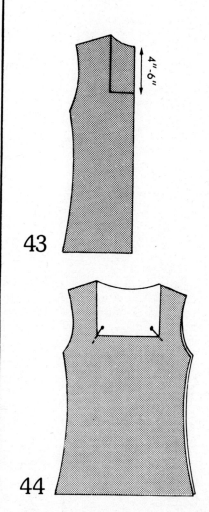

**43**

**44**

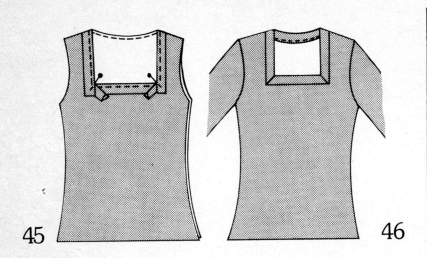

45                                                      46

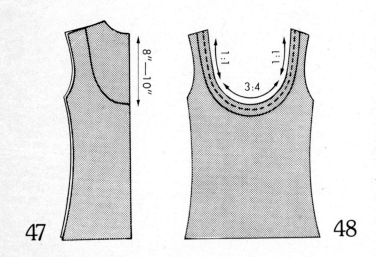

47                                                      48

The longer strip should be attached with a 1:1 ratio along the vertical edges of the square and a 3:4 ratio on the back neck edge between the shoulder seams. A 1-inch extension should be left at the corners. Fold the tabs from the strip at the lower edge out of the way before stitching the long strip. (Fig. 45) Finish the miter at the corners and complete the knit top as previously described, omitting the inset. (Fig. 46)

### RIB KNIT TRIM ON MITERED SQUARE-NECK TOP WITHOUT AN INSET

When you choose to sew the mitered square-neck without an inset and want to use rib knit for the trim, stretch the trim slightly across the sides and the lower edge of the square and use a 2:3 ratio of trim to neck edge across the back of the neck.

### U-NECK TOP WITH AN INSET

Fold the garment front exactly in half to cut the U. Measure down the center front fold 8 to 10 inches and connect this point to the middle of the shoulder with a curved line. A fashion ruler will help you draw the correct curve. (Fig. 47) Cut away the U-shaped piece, starting at the folded edge. Save this piece to use as a pattern for the inset.

Cut a strip of self-trim 2 to 2-1/2 inches wide. Measure the distance around the U and add 1 to 2 inches for the length of the trim. This will be slightly more trim than necessary but it's better to have a little extra than not enough. Fold and press the trim in half lengthwise and position it on the right side of the garment front with the cut edges together. Stitch with a 1/4-inch seam allowance, using a 1:1 ratio on the straight edges and a 3:4 ratio through the curve of the U. (Fig. 48) Turn the trim up into its finished position and press.

Use the U-shaped piece as a pattern for your inset, adding 1/2 inch on the edges of the U for seam allowances. The neck and shoulder edges should remain the same. (Fig. 49)

Place the inset beneath the wrong side of the front, matching the edge of the inset to the trim seam allowance. From the right side, pin the inset to the front along the folded edge of the trim. (Fig. 50) Turn the garment back to expose the previous stitching line and sew over it, including the inset piece in the stitching. Then, complete your knit top by following the instructions previously given in this chapter. (Fig. 51)

## U-NECK TOP WITH RIB KNIT FOR TRIM ON THE U

For this top, stretch the rib knit slightly along the straight edges and with a 2:3 ratio along the curve of the U. Then the ribbing will hug close to the body.

## U-NECK TOP WITHOUT AN INSET

If you prefer the neck finish to fall from the natural neckline rather than from slightly above it, cut 3/4 inch away from the <u>total</u> neck edge, front and back, before beginning. Fold the garment front exactly in half to cut the U. Measure down the center front fold 4 to 6 inches, depending on the depth of the neckline you choose. Connect that point to the shoulder neck edge with a curved line. A fashion ruler is a useful tool in drawing this curved line. (Fig. 52)

Sew the shoulder seams. Cut a strip of self-trim that measures 2 to 2-1/2 inches wide. The length of trim should be three-fourths the length of the total neck edge plus approximately 2 inches. This will allow you to use a 3:4 ratio at the back neck edge and through the curve of the

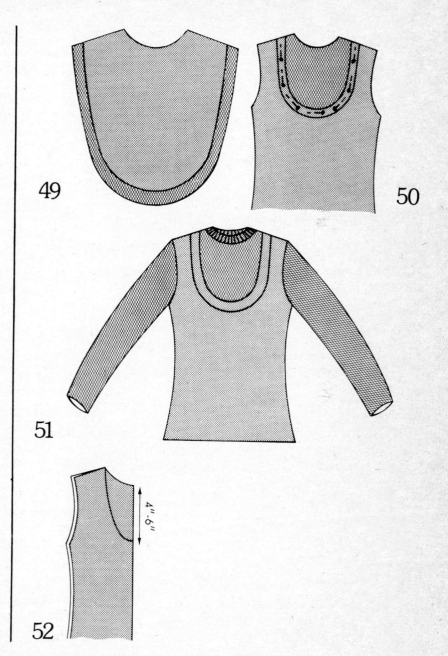

49

50

51

52

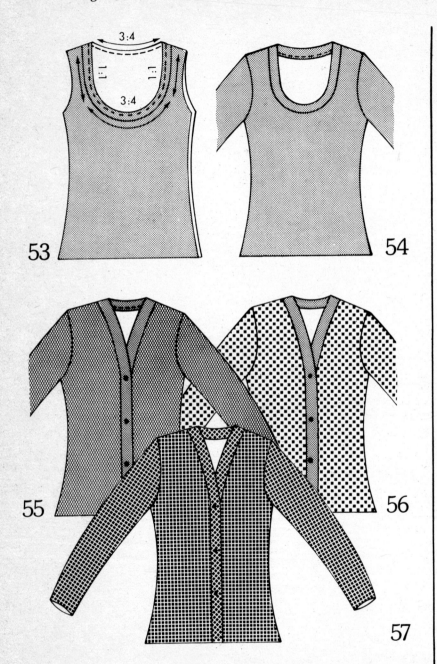

53

54

55

56

57

U with a 1:1 ratio along the straighter edges. Sew the two short ends of trim together to form a cylinder and lightly press it lengthwise, wrong sides together. Apply the trim to the neck edge with the proper ratio. (Fig. 53)

Complete the top according to the instructions given earlier in this chapter and you will have a garment that is attractive for casual or more formal occasions, depending on the fabric you have selected. (Fig. 54)

### RIB KNIT TRIM ON U-NECK TOP WITHOUT AN INSET

When you are sewing a U-neck without an inset and choose to use rib knit for the trim, stretch it slightly as you sew along the straight edges and use a 2:3 ratio through the curve of the U and across the back of the neck. This will cause the rib to hug close to the body.

# Cardigan Jacket with a Self-Trim Band
## Fabric

A medium to heavyweight fabric is usually best for this garment, although I have seen some lightweight fabrics used quite successfully. Cotton double knits, acrylics, and polyesters all lend themselves to this style.

One of the pleasures in creating your own fashion is combining colors and patterns in interesting ways. While the cardigan jacket is beautiful trimmed in self-fabric, you might consider using contrasting colors (Fig. 55) or a print with a plain-colored band. (Fig. 56) An effective use of plain or checked fabric is to cut strips on the bias for the banded trim. (Fig. 57) You will have an attractive outfit if you coordinate a jacket with a mitered V-neck top.

## Preparing Your Pattern

Since you are making a jacket, a garment which will be worn over another garment, trace your knit top pattern one size larger than your full bust size. Because your finished band will be 1-1/2 inches wide, cut 1-1/2 inches away from the back neck edge. (Fig. 58) Trace and cut the front pattern piece on the foldline. You will work with only half the front for this design. Remove 1/2 inch along the center front line. (Fig. 59) However, if you are especially full through the bust, you may wish to leave this 1/2 inch for the extra width you will need.

Measure 1-1/2 inches out on the shoulder seam and connect this point on the shoulder to a point 6-1/2 inches down the front from the neck edge. (Fig. 60) You can adjust the depth of your V to lower than 6-1/2 inches if you prefer. Remember that a trim of 1-1/2 inches will be added.

To provide extra width to your sleeve pattern, extend the lower edge 1 inch horizontally on each side and connect these points to the underarm. (Fig. 61)

## Cutting and Sewing Your Garment

Cut one back, two fronts, and two sleeves from your fabric, using your newly designed pattern. With right sides together, sew the two front pieces to the back at the shoulder seams. Here and elsewhere, you will be using 1/4-inch seams unless otherwise specified.

Cut two strips of self-, contrasting, or rib trim 3-1/2 inches wide for the bands. For length, measure on your pattern piece from the hemline

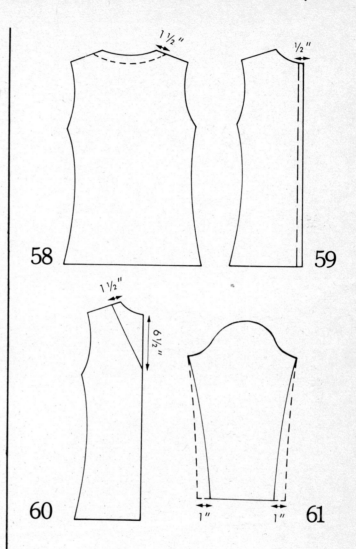

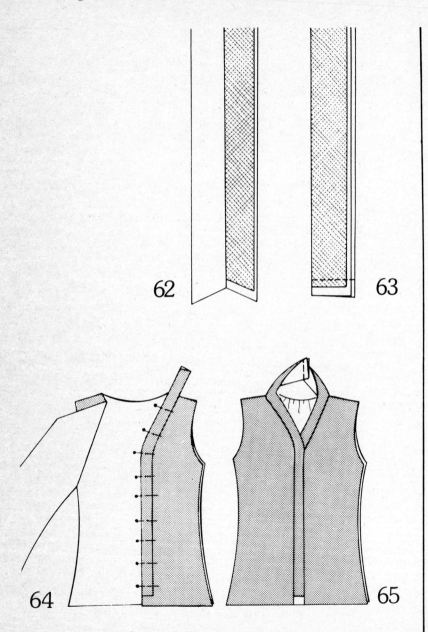

62

63

64

65

up the center front to the center back of the neck and add approximately 1-1/2 inches. Press the strips in half lengthwise with the wrong sides together.

For button and buttonhole reinforcement, cut two strips of *Perky Bond Plus* fusible interfacing fabric, each measuring 1-5/8 inches wide by the length of the front edge from the hemline to the point of the V. Each strip of *Perky Bond Plus* should be bonded inside a strip of banding so it will lie on the underside when the jacket is completed. (Fig. 62)

With right sides together, sew across the lower edge of each strip of banding, using a 1/4-inch seam allowance. (Fig. 63) Turn the strips of banding to the right side and press them carefully.

Pin the strips to the right side of the jacket front with all the cut edges even and the finished edge of each strip positioned at the hemline. (Fig. 64) With a 1:1 ratio, stitch each front edge from the lower edge up to 1 inch below the shoulder seam, allowing the extra banding to hang free.

Measure the back neck edge on the seamline between the points where you stopped stitching. Subtract 1-1/2 to 3 inches from this measurement, depending on the stretch of your banding fabric. The more stretch it has, the more you should subtract. Divide the measurement in half and add 1/4 inch for seam allowance. Measure each extending section of trim and cut it to equal this final measured length.

Open the two sections of banding and sew them, right sides together, with a 1/4-inch seam allowance. (Fig. 65) Press the seam allowance open and fold the banding again, wrong sides together. Pin the strip of banding to the neck edge, matching the seamline to the center back.

Complete the stitching, stretching the band to match the neck edge.

Finish the back neck edge from shoulder seam to shoulder seam by topstitching on the right side 1/8 inch beneath the banding seamline. The seam allowance should be caught in the topstitching for a neat appearance inside. (Fig. 66)

To finish the bands at the lower edge, turn each band so that it lies right sides together with the garment front. Fold the hem allowance over each one so that the band is sandwiched between the front and the hem allowance. Sew over the previous stitching line. (Fig. 67) Turn the hem to the inside and the seam will be enclosed. (Fig. 68)

Stretch the sleeves into the garment by first pinning at the underarm points and by matching the center of the sleeve cap to the shoulder seam. Sew with the garment on the top and the sleeve on the bottom next to the machine.

Finish the underarm seams by stitching from the lower edge of the garment up and out to the sleeve edge. Hem the sleeves and the lower edge with *Perky Bond*, with a machine stitch, or with a hand catchstitch.

This banded jacket (Fig. 69) is a great combination with any knit top, and it's especially nice over the mitered V-neck top with an inset.

## Variations

### CARDIGAN JACKET WITH A ONE-INCH BAND

The previous instructions were for a finished band of 1-1/2 inches wide. If you prefer a narrower band on your jacket, cut 1 inch away from the back neck edge. (Fig. 70)

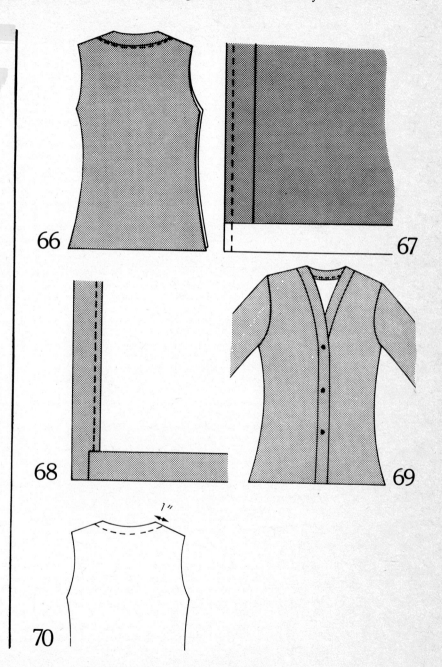

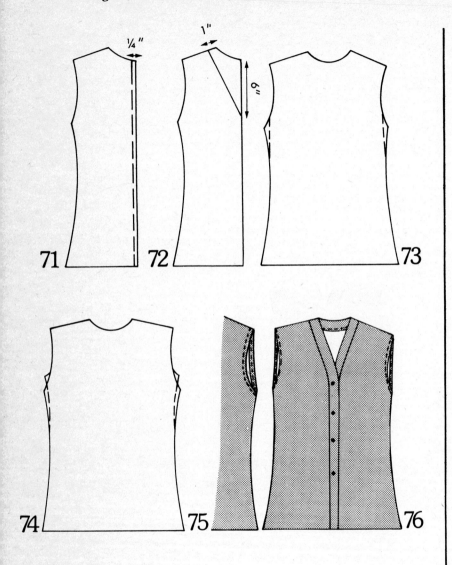

Using half the pattern front, trim away 1/4 inch from the center front line. (Fig. 71) Measure out on the shoulder 1 inch, depending on the amount you trimmed on the back neck edge, and connect this point to a point approximately 6 inches down from the center front edge. (Fig. 72) You can lower the depth of the V if you prefer. Remember that a 1-inch wide band will be added. This will be your front pattern piece.

The strips for the banding should measure 2-1/2 inches in width. Construct the jacket according to the instructions given above.

## BANDED CARDIGAN VEST

If you would like a banded cardigan vest, you must first trim the top corner of your pattern at the armscye. (Fig. 73) The knit top patterns were designed for a sleeve but with this simple alteration, a garment to be worn over another will hug closer to the body at the underarm as it should. For a sleeveless top to be worn by itself, you will need to raise the underarm about 3/4 inch in addition to trimming the top corner. (Fig. 74)

After you have completed the neck and front edges according to the previous instructions, sew the side seams. Turn the armscye seam 1/4 inch to the inside of the garment and topstitch 1/8 inch from the fold to finish the edge. (Fig. 75)

This vest (Fig. 76) is attractive worn over a body suit, body blouse, or knit top.

## BANDED CARDIGAN VEST
## WITH ARMSCYE FACING

For your vest, you might prefer an armscye finished without the topstitching. If that is the case, you will need to design a facing. The first step is to trim or fold back the extending corner from the top of the side seam of your pattern at the armscye as described above. (Fig. 77) Draw a line on your pattern front and back 2 to 2-1/2 inches inside the curve of the armscye. (Fig. 78) Trace these small sections from your pattern pieces and cut two of each from your fabric for the facings. Or, to eliminate bulk at the shoulder, lap the seam allowance of the front and back facing pattern pieces at the shoulder when cutting your facings.

After you have completed the neck and front edges and sewn the side seams of the vest according to the previous instructions, sew the facing pieces together at the underarm and, if necessary, at the shoulder. Apply them to the vest, right sides together, matching up the seamlines. After stitching, fold each facing to the inside and press it carefully. Hand-tack or bond the facings with *Perky Bond* to the seam allowances at the shoulder and underarm.

## A SLEEVELESS COAT WITH SELF-TRIM BAND

Use the Basic Dress Pattern 1500 for your master pattern. Cut and sew this pattern the same way as described for the vest. (Fig. 79) This sleeveless coat worn over the basic dress would be a nice addition to any woman's wardrobe.

In this chapter you have learned a variety of ways to apply several exciting techniques. You will enjoy using these same techniques in designing other garments.

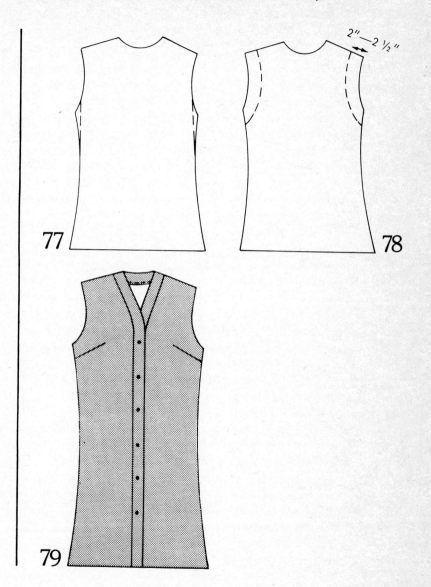

# 2

# Women's Jeans with a Yoke

# Women's Jeans with a Yoke

The Slacks and Shorts Pattern 700 has been a favorite since the beginning of Stretch & Sew. Two of the attractive features of this pattern are its simple design and easy construction. Now we have the Jeans Pattern 710 for women, which has a more tailored line achieved by the addition of pockets and a fly front closure.

Fashion seems to be constantly changing. As soon as we become accustomed to a certain style, a new look emerges and we are amazed to realize that our tastes have swung with the trend. We are suddenly ready for the new look!

The style variations that you can adapt to the Jeans Pattern will start you on your way to a wardrobe of pants appropriate for many occasions. While I am including several style changes in this chapter, you may select any one of them or any combination to get the look you want. Remember, too, that the ideas in *The Stretch & Sew Pants Book* may also be used effectively with this pattern.

## Patterns for These Techniques

*Jeans Pattern 710*
*Tennis Shorts Pattern 650*
*Slacks and Shorts Pattern 700*
*Infants' Combination Pattern 850*
*Children's Straight and Bell-Bottom Pants Pattern 860*
*Boys' Pants Pattern 925*
*Slacks and Shorts Pattern 1700*
*Slacks and Shorts Pattern 1701*
*Tennis Shorts Pattern 1720*
*Queen Size Pants Pattern 3700*
*Skirt with Darts and Waistband Pattern 450*

## General Fabric Selection

You will want your jeans to look crisp and tailored when they are completed. Many fabrics are appropriate for pants, but the style we are working with here calls for fairly firm fabric with approximately 25 percent stretch. If you select fabric with greater or lesser stretch, your pattern will have to be adjusted accordingly.

Don't forget the possibilities that are open to you in mixing coordinate fabrics. One idea is to select a plaid fabric for the main portion of the pants and to use a coordinate in a solid color for the yoke and pocket pieces. (Fig. 1) Let this start you thinking about interesting combinations for versatility in the use of fabric.

## Preparing Your Pattern

Start with the pattern that you have traced from the master pattern. Then, make any necessary alterations before you start making adjustments for fashion changes. It's a good idea to trace a second pattern from your altered pattern so that you will still have the original one when you need it.

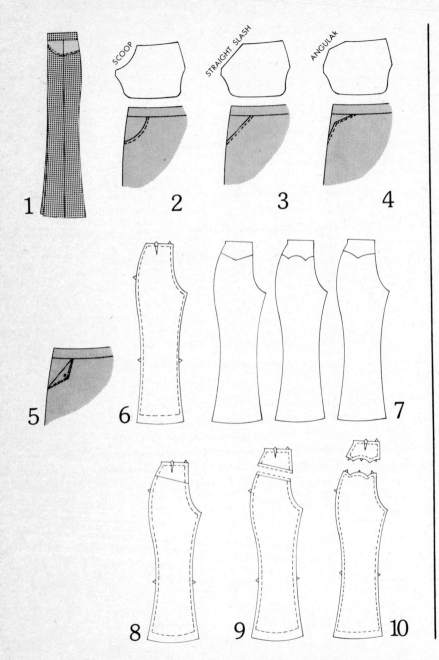

1   2   SCOOP   3   STRAIGHT SLASH   4   ANGULAR

5   6   7

8   9   10

A continental pocket is a favorite for pants. The Jeans Pattern comes with a scoop pocket that is very attractive. (Fig. 2) However, if you would like to vary this design, you may easily do so by tracing a new pocket pattern. You may change the curve to a straight slash (Fig. 3), or you may prefer an angular design with the corner extending up (Fig. 4), or turned down and finished with a button. (Fig. 5) This simple procedure will help you to style jeans uniquely yours.

You can add a yoke to the back of your jeans to complement the design of the continental pocket. First, mark all the seam allowances on your pattern with a dotted line and indicate the natural waistline and the hemline. (Fig. 6) Then, draw the yoke style you would like on your pattern. You can create a variety of looks. (Fig. 7) Usually it is best not to drop the <u>lowest point</u> of the yoke more than 2 inches beneath the <u>level</u> of the opening of the continental pocket on the side.

As an example, for an attractive but simple yoke, measure down 3 inches on the side seam from the waist edge and angle the yoke to a 6-inch drop at the center back. (Fig. 8) Or, measure on your front pattern piece to determine where the pocket joins the side seam to plan your yoke so the topstitching on the yoke will meet the topstitching on the pocket in front for an especially well-planned look.

Cut your pattern at the yoke line and add a 5/8-inch seam allowance to each cut edge. (Fig. 9) If you have drawn a complicated yoke, position some notches on the pattern pieces to ensure that you properly assemble them. (Fig. 10)

You may prefer to eliminate the darts in your yoke. If that is the case, you must do so <u>before</u>

you add a seam allowance to the cut edges of the pattern pieces along the yoke line. Extend the center dart line of each dart to the lower cut edge of the yoke. Cut on this line and close the dart so that the legs of the dart match at the seamline along the upper edge. The legs of the dart will not match along their entire length.

Tape your lapped pattern paper in place and add seam allowance to each cut edge along your yoke line. This procedure will shift the angle of the yoke line slightly, but you will have the proper shaping when the yoke pieces are sewn to the pants.

## Cutting and Sewing Your Garment

From your fabric, cut two fronts, two backs, two continental pocket pieces, two yoke pieces, and one waistband. You will also need a zipper guard which is 4-1/2 inches by 11 inches and one or more belt loops which are 1 inch wide and 1-1/2 inches longer than the width of your elastic. Cut a strip of Stretch & Sew waistband elastic 2-1/2 inches shorter than the length of the waistband piece. From *Perky Bond Plus* cut two interfacings for the halves of your pocket pieces which will lie on the underside. Trim 3/8 inch from all edges except the ones which will be placed against the foldlines.

Once you've cut your fabric and begin construction, keep in mind that you will be using 5/8-inch seam allowances throughout unless otherwise specified.

If you like, you may crease your pants before you begin sewing. Match the cut edges of each piece and, using a damp pressing cloth, press a crease up to the level of the crotch curve. If you prefer, you may wait until you have sewn the leg seams or until you have completely assembled the pants before putting in your creases.

A pocket is applied to each front section. Fold each pocket in half, right sides together, matching the side edges. Press each pocket to establish a foldline. Bond the interfacings to the underpockets and stitch the *Perky Bond Plus* to the pockets 1/8 inch from the foldlines.

With right sides together, position the open pocket on the pants front, matching the placement markings (Fig. 11) and stitch 5/8 inch from the edge of the pocket opening. (Fig. 12) Trim away the pants fabric above the pocket even with the pocket's cut edge. (Fig. 13) Then, trim the curve of the pocket seam allowance back to 1/4 inch. When you are using the angular design, cut a wedge from the seam allowance at the outside corner. (Fig. 14) Fold the pocket to the wrong side and press, rolling the seam slightly to the inside. Topstitch 1/4 inch from the edge. (Fig. 15)

Fold the pocket on the crease line so that the sides of the pocket and pant leg are even. Stitch the cut edges of the pocket's lower edge with a straight stitch and reinforce the seam with a zigzag stitch. (Fig. 16) Then, pin the pocket carefully into place and baste it to the pants at the waist edge and at the side. (Fig. 17)

Now you are ready to make your fly. So often, home sewers are afraid that this will be a difficult technique and are hesitant to try it. You will find that it is quite simple — and even fun — to put in a fly!

Place the front sections right sides together and sew between the two large dots at the lower edge of the fly facings. A second row of stitching

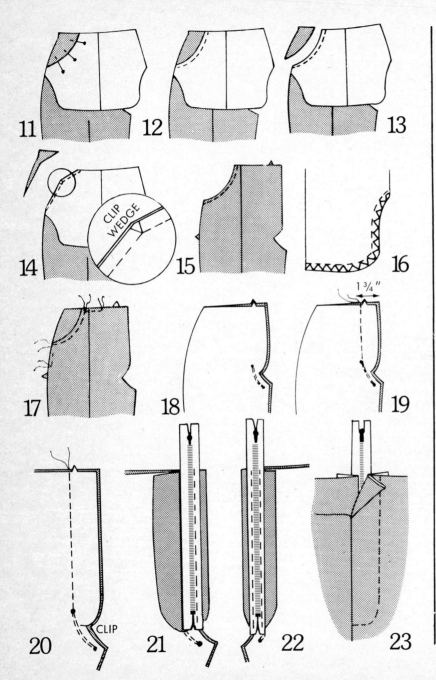

11  12  13
14  CLIP WEDGE  15  16
17  18  1 3/4"  19
20  CLIP  21  22  23

1/16 inch from the first is necessary to reinforce this stress point. (Fig. 18) With a machine basting stitch, continue sewing to the top of the pants 1-3/4 inches away from the edge. (Fig. 19) Then, clip into the seam at the lower edge of the fly facings. (Fig. 20)

Fold the fronts and the left fly facing to one side. Position the zipper face down on the right fly facing section with the metal stop even with the upper dot and the edge of the zipper tape against the basted seam. Using the zipper foot on your machine, sew along the right side of the zipper next to the zipper teeth. Stitch only through the zipper tape and the right fly facing section. (Fig. 21)

Fold the fronts to the other side and position the unstitched side of the zipper flat against the left fly facing. Sew along the left side of the zipper tape next to the zipper teeth, stitching only through the zipper tape and left fly facing. (Fig. 22)

Position the left fly facing section so that it is flat against the left front and topstitch through both thicknesses. Start by forming a curve at the bottom of the zipper. You might find it easier if you shorten your stitch length for this curved portion. The remainder of the stitching should be 1-1/4 inches from the center front. Remove the basting stitches from the center front seam (Fig. 23) and press the fly carefully.

Fold the zipper guard lengthwise with the wrong sides together and press. A strip of *Perky Bond* inserted into the fold before you press will offer more stability to the zipper guard and make it easier to apply.

Place the zipper guard behind the open zipper on the right fly facing section, matching the cut edges of the zipper guard to the cut edge of the facing. Using a zipper foot, topstitch 1/8 inch from the zipper teeth. (Fig. 24) Close the zipper and lift the pants, exposing the end of the zipper and the fabric guard. Sew across the zipper through all thicknesses and trim any extending fabric to 1/2 inch. (Fig. 25) You will trim away the excess zipper at the top <u>after</u> you have sewn on your waistband.

Your zipper is complete and you are ready to go on with your pants construction!

If you have left the darts in your yoke pieces, sew them at this time and press them towards the center back. (Fig. 26)

Then, with right sides together, sew the yoke pieces to the pants with a 5/8-inch seam allowance. If you drew the yoke with an angular design, it will be necessary to clip into the seam allowance at each pivot point in the seamline in order to release pulling in the seam allowance.

Topstitching the yoke after it has been sewn to the pants can be very attractive. Try using thread of a contrasting color for an added dimension. In determining the direction to press the seam allowances before topstitching, I follow the way of least resistance. In the case of a straight yoke line, they may be pressed either up or down, according to your preference. If you have planned the yoke and the topstitching to match the front pockets, press the seam allowances down and topstitch 1/4 inch from the seamline. (Fig. 27)

Pin the outside leg seams with the right sides of the front and back sections together, matching notches. It is important to place a pin every 6 to

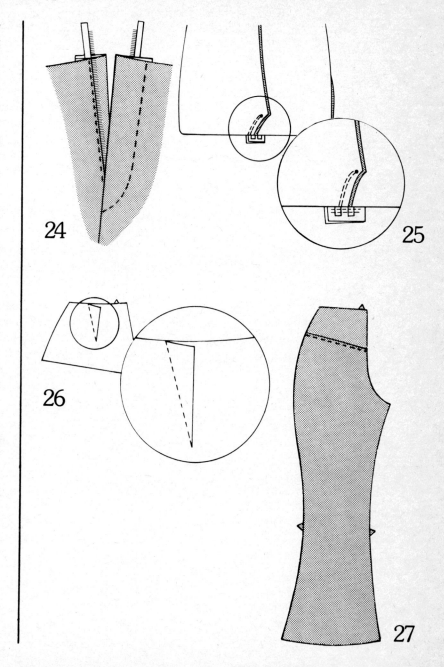

24

25

26

27

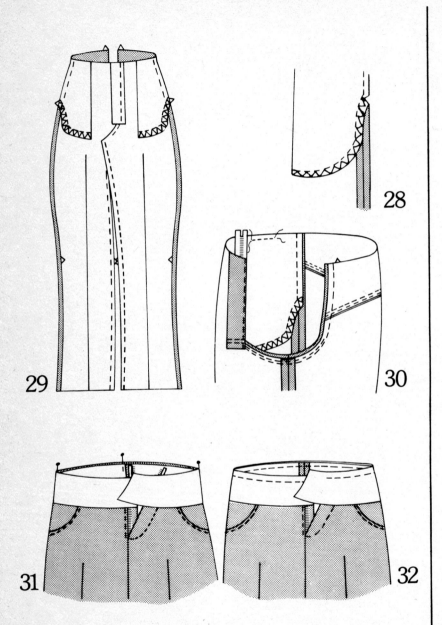

28

29

30

31

32

8 inches to be sure that you stretch evenly as you sew. Stitch the side seams, starting at the lower edge and continuing to the waist edge.

Clip the seam allowance at the lower edge of each pocket and press the side seams open below this point. (Fig. 28) The portion above the clip should be pressed toward the back. Before continuing, steam the excess fullness in the hip area, gently shrinking and easing the fabric.

Pin the inside leg seams, matching the notches, and sew from the lower edge to the crotch, stretching as you sew. (Fig. 29) Then, press the seams open.

Turn one pant leg right side out and place it inside the other leg so that they are right sides together. Match the cut edges of the crotch and sew, starting in the front where the previous stitching ended and stretching as you sew. This is a stress seam, so a second stitching through the lower part of the curve is advisable 1/8 inch from the first stitching line. Then, trim the seam to 1/4 inch in the lower part of the curve. (Fig. 30) Press the remaining center back seam open.

The waistband is applied to the pants by pinning it to the waist edge with right sides together, matching all the notches. The waistband will extend 3-5/8 inches beyond the center front of the left side. (Fig. 31)

When you sew the waistband to the pants, be sure the zipper is open. Stitch carefully over the zipper teeth, hand-wheeling the machine so you do not break the needle. As you sew, ease the fullness of the pants into the waistband piece. Trim the zipper even with the waistband seam allowance. (Fig. 32)

To prepare the elastic before sewing it to the waist edge, cut a piece of fleece, lining fabric, or pants fabric that is 4 inches long and as wide as the elastic. Fold it in half and lap the cut ends 1/4 inch over one end of the elastic and zigzag them together. (Fig. 33) This end of your elastic will be attached to the left front of the waistband.

Pin the elastic to the waistband seam allowance. The elastic should be positioned 5/8 inch inside the right end of the waistband and the fleece or fabric extension should be positioned 5/8 inch inside the left end of the waistband. (Fig. 34) Stitch with a zigzag stitch.

Fold the waistband lengthwise with the right sides together and sew across each end. (Fig. 35) Do not include the elastic or the fleece in the stitching. Turn the waistband right side out, folding it firmly over the elastic. Then, stitch-in-the-ditch from the right side along the waistband seam, taking care when you sew over the zipper. (Fig. 36) Trim close to the stitching line on the inside and clip to the seamline at the beginning of the waistband tab.

You complete the waistband tab by tucking the seam allowance up into the tab and slipstitching it closed by hand. (Fig. 37) For the waistband closure, a combination of a pant hook and button works very well. Place a hook directly above the zipper and a button closure at the end of the tab.

You may choose to use only one belt loop, attaching it to the waistband 1-1/2 to 2 inches to the right of the center front. Or, you may choose to put belt loops around the waistband of the jeans, placing one in the center back, one on each side, and one about 2 inches on either side of the center front.

Cut the belt loops 1 inch wide and 1-1/2 inches longer than the width of your waistband elastic. (You may cut a wider belt loop according

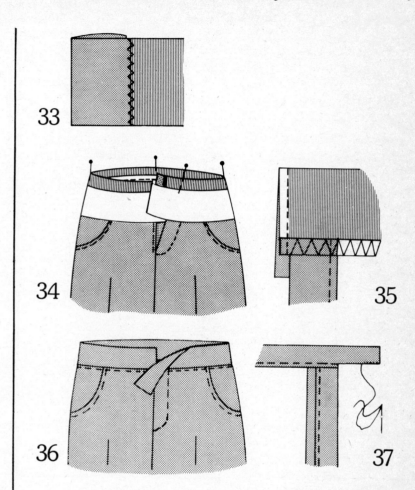

33

34

35

36

37

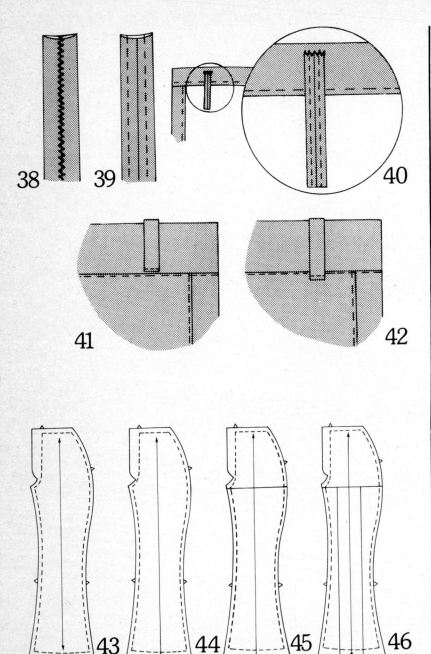

to your fashion preference.) Fold each strip in thirds lengthwise with the right side out and sew along the center with a small zigzag stitch (Fig. 38) or with two lines of straight stitching. (Fig. 39) Or bond them with small strips of *Perky Bond.*

Attach the belt loops by placing the right side of one end against the wrong side of the waistband approximately 1/2 inch from the top and sewing it with a zigzag stitch. (Fig. 40) Turn the belt loop over to the right side, fold the unfinished end under, and stitch it to the waistband (Fig. 41) or just below the waistband. (Fig. 42)

Hem the pant legs and you'll be so excited about your new jeans with their fashion flair!

# Variations

### SLASHING AND SPREADING FOR A FULLER LEG

The Jeans Pattern is designed with a slight flare below the knee. If you prefer, you may slash the pattern and spread it for additional flare.

For a leg that is flared from the hip, draw in the seamlines on your pattern pieces. (Fig. 43) Extend the straight-of-grain line to the waist and lower edges. (Fig. 44) Then, draw a line across the pattern pieces just below the crotch shelf. (Fig. 45)

The straight-of-grain line will be your center slash line. Draw two other lines so that each one is centered between the middle line and the seamline. (Fig. 46) Cut and spread each slash line 3/4 inch.

As you spread the pattern, you will need to cut on the horizontal line or fold tucks at the top of each slash, whichever seems easier for you. The seams will be shortened slightly but this is usually necessary to create a well-balanced curve at the hem. (Fig. 47)

Remember to follow the same steps for the front and back pattern pieces, spreading each slash an equal amount. Back the slashes with *Perky* Pattern Paper or *Do-Sew* pattern material. You may redraw your pattern if you wish.

## YOKE TECHNIQUE USED ON THE LEG

Follow the same procedure for a design on the pant legs as you did for a yoke. This is an attractive variation on a straight or flared leg. Remember to add seam allowance to the cut edges of the pattern before you cut your fabric. Topstitching or the use of contrasting fabrics lends an interesting touch. (Fig. 48)

## PATCH POCKETS

Patch pockets are a nice addition to pants. If you are not using the yoke variation, you might want to sew patch pockets to the back of your jeans. Start with the pocket piece that is included in the pattern and reshape the lower edge in any way that you like. (Fig. 49) Or you might prefer to use the pattern piece exactly as it was designed for you.

You may stabilize your pockets by interfacing them with *Perky Bond Plus*. Cut the *Perky Bond Plus* 3/8 inch smaller all the way around than your pocket piece and bond the two together before continuing with construction.

Press each pocket along the foldline at the top with the right sides together (Fig. 50), and stitch the 5/8-inch seamline on the sides and lower edge

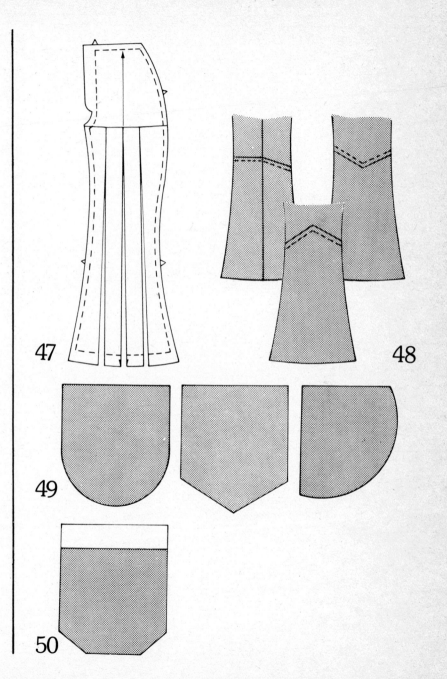

47

48

49

50

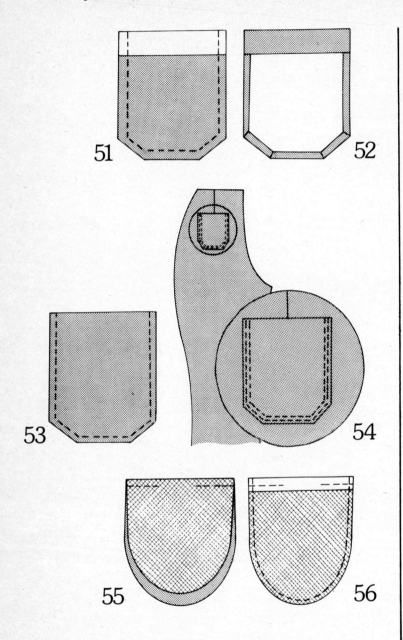

to establish an accurate foldline for the pocket seam allowance. (Fig. 51) Trim the upper corners and turn the top of the pocket right side out. Press the seam allowance to the wrong side along the stitching line, folding the corners so the fabric will lie flat. (Fig. 52)

Topstitch 1/4 inch from the pocket edge on three sides and press. (Fig. 53) Pin each pocket to the back of the pants according to the placement marks on the pattern and stitch 1/8 inch from the pocket edge, reinforcing the top corner. (Fig. 54)

## PATCH POCKET VARIATION

This second method for applying patch pockets provides an especially smooth finish, and the inside of the pocket will be free of seam allowance!

Start with a square of fabric that measures approximately 6-1/4 inches wide by 7 inches long. Shape the lower half or the top any way you like. Using the same pattern, cut a pocket lining from *Perky Bond Plus*, but subtract 3/4 inch from the top and 1/8 inch from the sides.

Place the non-adhesive side of the *Perky Bond Plus* against the right side of the pocket. Stitch across the upper edge, easing the extra pocket fabric into the lining. Leave 1-1/2 inches open in the center for turning. (Fig. 55) Pull the lining down to match the edges of the pocket. This will provide a fold at the top of the pocket and the seam will be 3/4 inch to the inside. Stitch the two pieces together with a 5/8-inch seam allowance. (Fig. 56)

Clip corners and trim the curves. Turn the pocket to the right side through the opening in the upper edge of the pocket. The edges of the pocket will turn under slightly due to the smaller size of the lining. Press the pocket carefully, using a damp cloth. Sew a line of topstitching around the entire pocket 1/4 inch from the edge. Then, stitch the pocket to the pants 1/8 inch from the pocket edge, reinforcing the upper corners.

## ADDING FEATURES FROM THE JEANS TO A SKIRT

You might enjoy sewing and wearing skirts, using the techniques that you have learned in this chapter for jeans. The Stretch & Sew Skirt Pattern 450 lends itself especially well to this.

Eliminate the center back seam when you trace your pattern by placing the seamline on a fold of pattern paper. (Fig. 57) You need to remove the darts on your front and back pattern pieces. Mark a point 5/8 inch out from the side of the pattern lower edge. Draw a straight line to connect this point to the side of the pattern at the hip (9 inches down from the waist). Then, mark a point 1-1/2 inches in from the side at the pattern upper edge. Draw a slightly curved line to connect this point to the side of the pattern at the hip, blending into the straight line. (Fig. 58) Sew the skirt along the new side seam and you will have the proper shaping at the waist without sewing darts.

Draw a yoke on the back pattern piece just as you did for the jeans. (Fig. 59) Don't forget to add seam allowance to each pattern cut edge.

You may make a fly front by putting a center front seam in your skirt. Cut your pattern on the foldline and add seam allowance to each cut edge. (Fig. 60) You must also add a fly facing to your pattern. Attach a strip of paper to the center front cut edge and measure out at the center front of

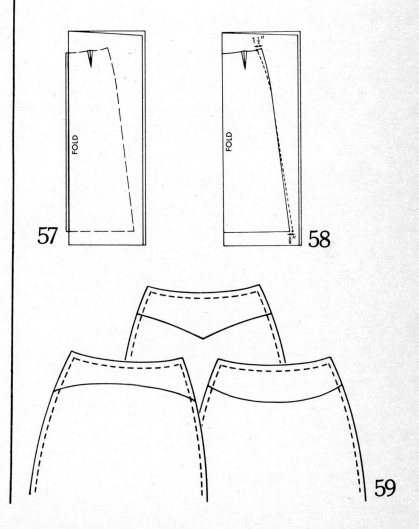

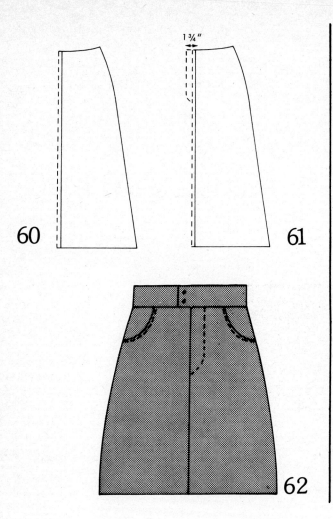

1 ¾"

60

61

62

your pattern 1-3/4 inches from the <u>seamline.</u> Draw a line approximately 8-1/2 to 9 inches straight down from this point and connect it to the pattern with a curved line. (Fig. 61) Your fly facing is completed! Sew your fly and zipper just as you would for the jeans.

Use the pocket pieces from the Jeans Pattern 710 for the continental pockets on your skirt, following the previous instructions for sewing them.

You will need additional length on your waistband piece to allow for a closure. Use the waistband from the Jeans Pattern or extend the length of the skirt waistband about 3 inches. Construct the waistband and apply it to the skirt as described for the jeans and you'll be done! (Fig. 62)

This is such a fun skirt and you designed it yourself. You have discovered just one of the ways of applying techniques described in this chapter.

# 3

# Relocating the Underarm Dart
# Adding Fullness to Sleeves

# Relocating the Underarm Dart Adding Fullness to Sleeves

Changing the basic design of a pattern is something many home sewers never think of doing. Techniques that are not commonly used at home sound difficult. But, in this chapter, I will be sharing with you an exciting yet simple method of relocating the underarm dart, the dart most often used in Stretch & Sew patterns. And, you will learn a number of ways to change a sleeve design in order to add variety to an otherwise basic pattern.

A dart gives fit to a garment, but it can also add to the design. Follow each step carefully as you relocate your dart. Once you understand the concepts, you will be able to apply them to any Stretch & Sew pattern that has a dart to create your own fashion.

You will enjoy using your imagination to combine dart variations and sleeve styles which complement one another. For example, a dart relocated to gathers at the neck edge in a dress with full sleeves presents a softly flattering picture — one of many possible looks.

## Patterns for These Techniques

*Basic Dress Pattern 1500*
*Shell Pattern 350*
*Body Blouse Pattern 790*
*Set-In Sleeve Jacket Pattern 1050*
*Fitted Basic Dress Pattern 1550*
*Shirtwaist Dress Pattern 1575*
*Queen Size Dress Pattern 3010*

## General Fabric Selection

Almost any knit fabric will sew beautifully into any of these garments. The fabric that you choose will determine whether it will be tailored and crisp or softly draped.

While most of these patterns may be used with fabric of any design, it is well to consider the finished look of the garment in relation to your dart relocation before cutting into your fabric. For example, if your fabric has a large floral pattern and you have relocated your underarm dart to a French dart, the dart might interrupt the design. In this case, it would be a better idea to relocate the dart to gathers. The French dart may be used effectively, however, with many vertically striped fabrics. The stripes will chevron to create a slimming line.

## Relocating the Underarm Dart

FLAT PATTERN METHOD

In designing there are two methods of developing a pattern. One is to work with the fabric and drape it on the body or a mannequin, pinning and cutting to achieve the design that you wish to create. This method is often used in the couturier houses, where only one garment will be made of a particular design.

The second method of developing a pattern, used in the pattern-making and garment industries, is flat pattern designing. This method was developed to make patterns and, ultimately, garments more uniform and consistent in fit.

For flat pattern designing, you begin with a basic pattern. The industry refers to this master pattern as a "sloper." In our work in this chapter, we will use the Stretch & Sew Basic Dress Pattern 1500 as our sloper. First, you will establish a perfect fit from that pattern and then, you will be able to create designs and fashions that meet your own desires.

When you think of the flat pattern method, I would like to have you think of a flat piece of paper that must take on the contours of the figure. The most important thing to remember is that the body has curves and the paper pattern is flat. As you make your design changes, slashes in the paper pattern will be made to allow it to lie flat.

A general rule in working with flat pattern designing is to remove seam allowances from your basic pattern before you begin and to add them back when your design is completed. This is necessary when slash lines will be drawn to a seam and you do not want to add length to your seamline.

I have never been able to keep a secret or miss the opportunity to share the things that I have learned along the way. Flat pattern designing is just one more thing that I feel many of you will enjoy learning about. Even if you never take a pair of scissors to a pattern, you will understand the patterns that you select better than you did before.

## ADJUSTING THE DART FOR A GOOD FIT

I will be using the Basic Dress Pattern 1500 throughout the chapter for the sake of example, but you should follow the same steps for any pattern with a dart. Before you relocate the underarm dart, you should adjust it to fit your figure. Trace half the front in the correct size from your master pattern onto *Perky* Pattern Paper or *Do-Sew* pattern material. Then, trace the dart and the box for altering.

Two body measurements are necessary to determine whether an alteration of the pattern dart is needed. On your body, measure across your bust from high point to high point. (Fig. 1) Divide the number of inches in half and, measuring in from the center front, indicate this point on your pattern piece. (Fig. 2)

Now, measure straight down from your shoulder to the high point of your bust. (Fig. 3) Be certain you are measuring straight down and not at an angle. On your pattern, measure down from the shoulder seamline on a line perpendicular to the previously determined horizontal point. Adjust the height of the horizontal point according to your vertical measurement and mark it on the pattern with a pencil dot. This is the high point of your bust. (Fig. 4)

Using the high point of the bust as your center point, draw a circle around it with a radius of 1, 1-1/2, or 2 inches. (The radius is the distance from a circle's center to its edge.) If you wear an A cup bra size, a radius of 1 inch is usually most flattering. If you wear a B cup size, a radius of 1-1/2 inches is correct. For a figure that requires a C or D cup size, a 2-inch radius is preferable. (Fig. 5)

When the center line of the dart is extended as shown, it should cross the high point of the bust. This indicates that the dart is correctly positioned. (Fig. 6) If necessary, redraw the lines to lengthen or shorten the dart so that the end of it just touches the edge of the circle.

If the center line, when extended, is above the high point (Fig. 7), the dart must be lowered. This is done by cutting along the top and down the side of the dart box, which is indicated on the pattern by a dotted line. Fold the pattern down until the dart is in the correct position. (Fig. 8)

If the extended center line of the dart is below the high point of the bust (Fig. 9), the dart must be raised. Cut along the bottom and up the side of the box and fold it as illustrated (Fig. 10) until the dart is correctly positioned.

When you have finished, tape a piece of paper behind the open area on the pattern so that it will be complete and easier to work with. Redraw the circle and, if necessary, redraw the lines to lengthen or shorten the dart so that the end of it just touches the edge of the circle. Now, you have a dart that will fit your figure exactly. (Fig. 11)

When you are certain of the fit of the dart, you may find it helpful to trace a new pattern with all of the adjustments included. This will give you a permanent pattern that will be useful for making many other dresses. Now, you are ready to move on to dart relocation.

## Relocating to Other Dart Styles

In the following section, three dart styles are described — the French dart, the armscye dart, and the shoulder dart. It is important to remember, however, that the procedure for relocating a

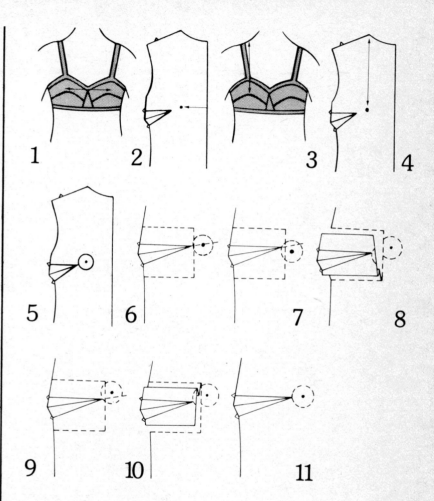

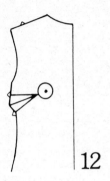

12

dart is the same no matter which dart style you select. Once you understand the techniques, you will be able to relocate to any type of dart, according to your desire.

To relocate a dart, you will begin by tracing half the front from your altered pattern onto a piece of *Perky* Pattern Paper or *Do-Sew*. You may use a whole pattern here, but you will be able to work more quickly with half a pattern. It is important that you draw the circle around the bust high point with the proper radius. (Fig. 12)

A basic concept to help you understand the procedure for relocating a dart is that there are two types of darts — a designer's dart and a dressmaker's dart. A designer's dart is drawn to the bust high point and provides a pivot point which allows you to keep the pattern flat when you are making style changes. A dressmaker's dart is drawn to the edge of the circle around your bust high point. This is the dart which you actually sew into the garment. It stops short of your bust high point for a more flattering appearance but it releases the fullness you need for a proper fit.

When you are relocating a dart, you will always need to extend the center line of the dressmaker's dart on the pattern to the bust high point. In this way, you restore the original center line of the designer's dart to provide the correct pivot point for dart relocation. After you have established your new dart, you will need to redraw the lines so that they stop at the edge of the circle. This will form the dressmaker's dart, which you will sew into the garment.

## FRENCH DART

The French dart is flattering to many people. Its diagonal line has a slimming and graceful effect.

Draw a line that you would like for your French dart. This line should extend from the bust high point diagonally to a point on the side seam below the underarm dart. (Fig. 13) A French dart which falls at the waistline or below is most flattering. Cut on the line you have drawn.

Place a ruler on the center line of the underarm dart and extend it to the bust high point to establish the center line of the designer's dart. (Fig. 14) Cut on this line. Then, close the underarm dart by pivoting the pattern paper at the bust high point, bringing the stitching lines of the underarm dart together at the side seam. (The legs of the dart will not match.) Tape the lapped paper in place.

When you closed the underarm dart, you opened the French dart. (Fig. 15) Back this open dart with *Perky* Pattern Paper, allowing extra paper to extend at the bottom. Tape this paper in place and carefully fold the dart down into position. This will establish a crease in the paper at the center of the dart like the center line of the original dart.

Trim the extra paper even with the side seam of the pattern. When you open the pattern, it will have the proper shaping so that the dart will be caught into the seamline after it has been sewn. (Fig. 16) Redraw the dart lines so that the point of the dart does not extend beyond the edge of the circle. This forms your dressmaker's dart. (Fig. 17)

Construct the dress according to the pattern instructions, sewing the dart in the new location.

## ARMSCYE DART

The armscye dart is often used in sleeveless garments such as jumpers, vests, and sleeveless

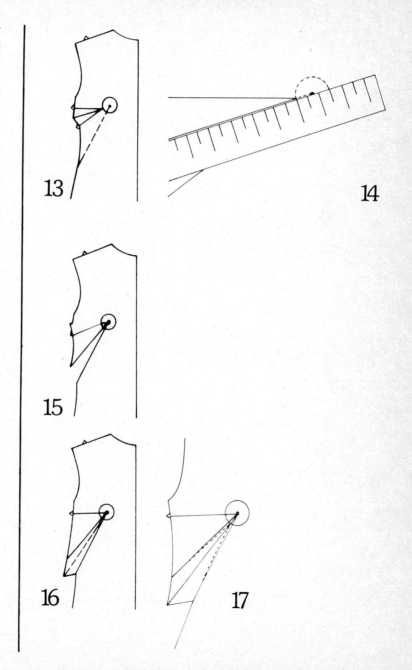

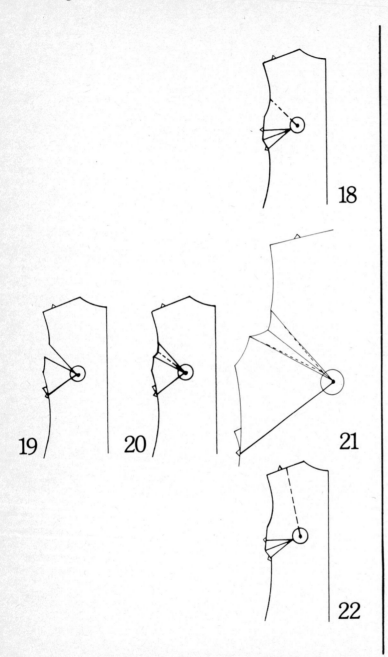

18

19

20

21

22

coats. It is also a favorite for maternity wear. You must follow the same steps to relocate the underarm dart to the armscye as you would to relocate to a French dart.

Start by drawing a line for your armscye dart. While you may draw this dart from any point on the armscye, it is generally located approximately 3 to 4 inches above the underarm. (Fig. 18) Extend the dart to the bust high point and cut on this line.

To open the armscye dart, close the underarm dart in the manner previously described for a French dart. (Fig. 19) Back the open dart with *Perky* Pattern Paper and fold it down to its proper position. Trim the excess paper even with the armscye edge so that the new dart will have the proper shaping to fit into the seamline when it is stitched. (Fig. 20) Then, redraw the dart so that the point extends only to the circle's edge to form your dressmaker's dart. (Fig. 21) Complete the dress according to the pattern instructions.

### SHOULDER DART

The shoulder dart is slimming because of its vertical line. It is used often in jackets and coats but it is sometimes used in dresses when another type of dart might disrupt the pattern of the fabric.

The procedure for relocating the underarm dart to a shoulder dart is the same as for a French dart or for an armscye dart. Start by drawing a shoulder dart line. It usually begins at the center of the shoulder and extends to the bust high point which, again, will serve as the pivot point for relocation. (Fig. 22)

Cut on the shoulder dart line and close the original underarm dart in the manner previously described for a French dart. Back the open dart with *Perky* Pattern Paper and fold it into place toward the center front. Then, cut the excess paper even with the shoulder edge of the pattern to give proper shaping to the dart. (Fig. 23) Redraw the shoulder dart so that the point extends only to the circle's edge to form your dressmaker's dart. (Fig. 24)

Now, you have relocated the underarm dart to the shoulder. Sew your dress according to the instructions given with the pattern.

## Relocating to Gathers

Soft gathers from the shoulder line or from the neck edge can be very flattering. Fabrics which drape well are especially appropriate with this technique. Start with half a pattern front traced from a pattern that has been adjusted to your figure.

### GATHERS FROM THE SHOULDER

For gathers that come from the shoulder, draw three lines from the shoulder edge to the bust high point. You should place the center line at the middle of the shoulder and the other two lines an equal distance from the center line but not in the neck or armscye seam allowance. (Fig. 25) Cut on these lines.

Close the underarm dart by extending the center line of the dart to the bust high point to establish the center line of the designer's dart. Cut on that line. Pivot the pattern paper at the bust high point so that the stitching lines of the underarm dart come together at the side seam. Then, tape the lapped dart in place.

Closing the underarm dart opened the three slashes at the shoulder. (Fig. 26) Place a piece of *Perky* Pattern Paper or *Do-Sew* behind the slashed

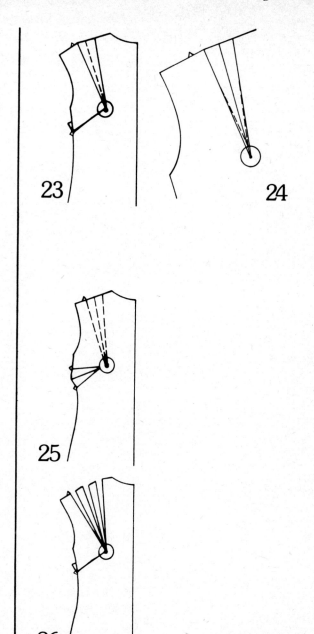

23

24

25

26

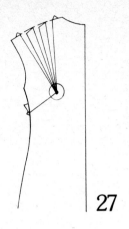

27

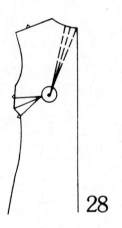

28

area and tape the pattern strips to it. The distance between the strips should be equally spaced. Connect the topmost points of each slashed section with a curved line. It would be helpful to use a fashion ruler. Use notches to mark the section of the shoulder seam which has been slashed and spread for gathers. (Fig. 27)

After cutting your fabric from the pattern, run two gathering lines between the notches on the shoulder, one 1/4 inch from the cut edge and the second 3/4 inch from the cut edge. Pull the stitches together so that the length of this seam is the same as it was on the original pattern.

Complete the dress according to the instructions enclosed with the pattern. As you sew the shoulder seam you must stretch — but don't stretch too hard. With a soft knit fabric, you could easily stretch the gathers out of the front section. Keep the gathers firmly in place by pinning them in several places to the back shoulder seam.

## GATHERS AT THE NECK EDGE

For gathers at the neck edge, follow the same basic steps as you did for gathers at the shoulder. Draw three lines from the neck edge to the bust high point. The first line should come from the center front, the second should be spaced 1 inch from the first line, and the third 1 inch from the second. (Fig. 28) Cut on these three lines.

Close the underarm dart in the manner described for relocating a dart to gathers at the shoulder, opening the slashes at the neck edge. Place a piece of *Do-Sew* or *Perky* Pattern Paper behind the slashes and tape the strips in place with each one an equal distance from the next. Connect the topmost points of each slashed section with a curved line. A fashion ruler would be helpful here. Use a notch to mark off the section of the neck edge which has been slashed and spread. (Fig. 29)

After cutting your fabric from the pattern, run two gathering lines between the notches at the neck edge, one 1/4 inch from the cut edge and the second 3/4 inch from the cut edge. Draw the threads together so that the length of the seam is the same as on the original pattern. Then, construct the garment by following the instructions with the pattern, taking care to keep the gathers firmly in place as you finish the neck edge.

Chanel trim at the neckline is especially attractive with gathers at the neck edge. If you decide on this finish, trim away the seam allowance before you gather, following the new neckline.

## Relocating to Yokes

The possibilities for yoke styles are practically unlimited. Your creative genius can go in many directions with this simple technique for truly original designs.

You may add a yoke to any garment by simply drawing the yoke line on the pattern, cutting it apart, and adding seam allowance to each cut edge as you did in Chapter Two. However, if you wish to incorporate the fit of the dart into a yoke, more care must be taken when you position the yoke line. The procedure is simple, but you must follow it carefully for the correct fit to result.

I will take you through each step for relocating the dart to one yoke design. But, you use these same steps for any yoke. So, be creative!

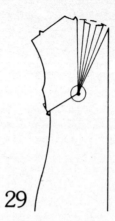

29

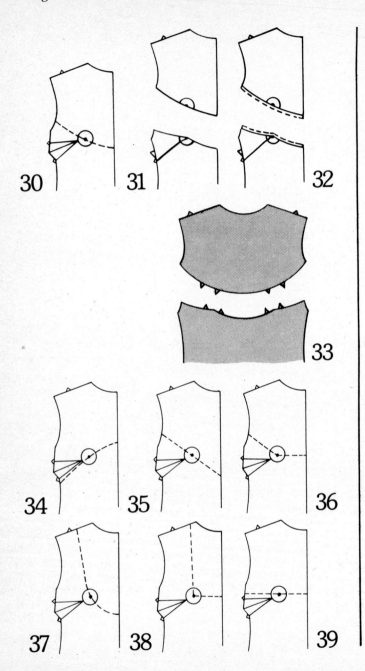

First, trace half a front from your pattern with the dart altered for your figure. On this fresh pattern, draw the yoke you would like, keeping in mind that this line <u>must</u> go through the bust high point. (Fig. 30) The yoke that I have chosen for illustration has a line that might be compared to an extension of the armscye dart.

Cut the pattern apart at the yoke line and close the underarm dart by cutting down the center line of the dart to the bust high point and pivoting the pattern paper. Match the stitching lines of the dart at the side seam and tape the lapped paper in place. (Fig. 31) Then, add a 5/8-inch seam allowance to each pattern piece at the yoke line. (Fig. 32)

Cut your fabric from this newly designed pattern, marking the points on your fabric with notches where the circle around each bust high point intersects the seamlines on the pattern pieces. (Fig. 33) You must line these notches up to each other when you stitch the yoke together so that the bust fullness will be correctly distributed. Complete your dress according to the pattern instructions.

There are many other yoke lines that are flattering to various figure types. If you have found the French dart to be good for your figure, try a yoke with a line similar to the French dart. (Fig. 34) The line of an armscye dart may be extended for a straight V-line yoke (Fig. 35) or it may be squared off at the bust line. (Fig. 36) The line of the shoulder dart is a good basis for the bib look in a U-shape (Fig. 37) or a square shape. (Fig. 38) The underarm dart line is very popular extended into a horizontal yoke line. (Fig. 39)

As you can see, there are many possibilities for yokes Follow each step described above and you will have your own creation. Interesting effects can always be achieved by combining fabrics — remember the coordinate fabrics for your yokes! And topstitching can be used to add variety and interest to your finished dress.

## Variations

### GATHERS FROM A DROPPED SHOULDER SEAM

Dropping the shoulder seam in the front before you relocate the underarm dart to gathers at the shoulder is very attractive. This creates a smooth finish over the shoulder with a yoke line and gathers over the bust. (Fig. 40)

First, draw the line for your new shoulder seam on your pattern front. It should be parallel to the original cut edge, approximately 2 to 2-1/2 inches below it. (Fig. 41) Cut on this line and add seam allowance to each cut edge. (Fig. 42) Then, position the small section on the back pattern piece, lapping the seam allowances. (Fig. 43)

Follow the previous instructions for relocating the dart to gathers at the shoulder, but use the new shoulder line. You will love this new style. It will be a creation uniquely yours!

### SCOOPED NECK WITH GATHERS

Follow the same steps if you would like a scooped neck with gathers as you did for gathers at the neck edge. Just lower the neckline of the pattern before you relocate the dart. (Fig. 44) This is only one of the many things that you can do with gathers in place of darts. Once you've done it, you will want to try your own ideas!

## Adding Fullness to Sleeves

The following information will make it possible for you to redesign a basic sleeve to any one

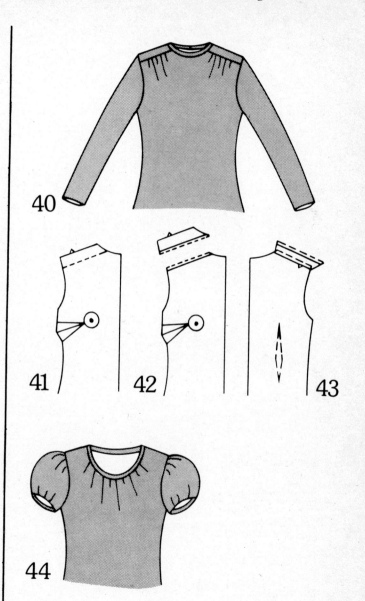

of the several styles which are described below. Once you understand the procedures involved, you will be able to create any sleeve style you'd like!

In order to add fullness to a sleeve, you must first have a sleeve pattern traced from your master pattern in the correct size. When you are slashing and spreading the sleeve for fullness but want to maintain the original fit where the sleeve joins the armscye, you must remove the seam allowance from the sleeve cap. If you slash and spread into the seam allowance, it will be necessary to gather the sleeve before setting it into the garment. After you have made all your pattern adjustments, redraw the sleeve cap seam allowance.

Another handy thing to remember is that the more fullness you want to add to a sleeve, the more slash lines you should draw. As a general rule, you will need one slash line for every 1-1/2 inches of fullness you add.

## LONG FULL SLEEVE WITH A FITTED CAP

The first step in designing this sleeve is to decide how you will finish the lower edge. If you want to add a cuff, you will want to shorten the sleeve pattern accordingly. If you would like the sleeve to blouse over the cuff, allow an extra 1 to 2 inches in length after you have subtracted the width of the cuff.

The 1-inch hem allowance will provide sufficient length to finish the sleeve with 1/4-inch or 3/8-inch elastic. Add 1 to 2 inches to the sleeve length if you would like the sleeve to blouse over the elastic at the wrist.

Remove the seam allowance from the sleeve cap and straighten the sleeve from the underarm points to the lower edge. (Fig. 45) Then, extend

45

the straight-of-grain line to the upper and lower edges of the sleeve pattern and draw equally spaced slash lines on either side of it. (Fig. 46) The more fullness you want, the more slash lines you should draw.

Cut on these lines and spread each section equally for the desired fullness. Place a piece of *Perky* Pattern Paper behind the sleeve and tape it in place. Then, redraw the line at the lower edge of the sleeve, using the curved edge of a fashion ruler to connect the topmost point of each slashed section. Now, replace the sleeve cap seam allowance. (Fig. 47)

If you did not add extra length to your sleeve pattern because you did not want the sleeve to blouse over the finish at the wrist, you will need to provide ease for your elbow. Using your fashion ruler, add 1 to 1-1/2 inches to the back of your sleeve at the lower edge as illustrated. (Fig. 48) Take care to keep your underarm seams the same length.

## LEG-OF-MUTTON SLEEVE

You might prefer a sleeve that has fullness added just through the sleeve cap. This is often referred to as the "leg-of-mutton" sleeve. For this look, you will add height as well as fullness to the sleeve cap. First, extend the straight-of-grain line to the upper edge of the sleeve pattern. Then, draw a horizontal line across your pattern, connecting the underarm points. (Fig. 49)

Draw three lines on each side of the straight-of-grain line for a total of seven vertical lines on the sleeve cap. (Fig. 50) If you'd like an extra full sleeve cap, you will need more than seven slash lines.

Cut on each line. Then, raise the sleeve cap about 2 to 3 inches and spread the sleeve sections,

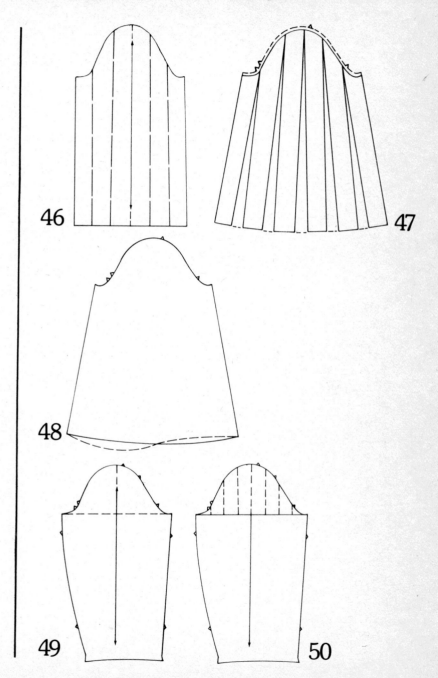

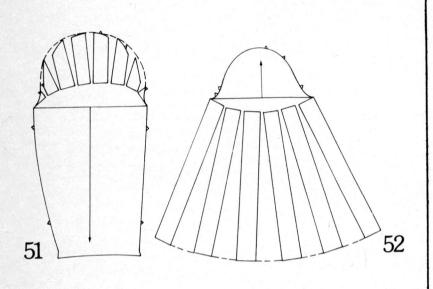

51

52

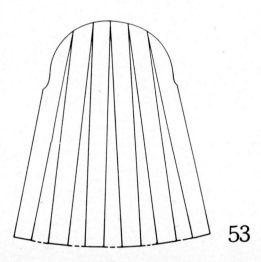

53

maintaining the position of the underarm points so that they will match the underarm points of the lower half of the sleeve pattern when the two sections are joined again. (Fig. 51)

Place a piece of *Perky* Pattern Paper behind the sleeve cap and tape the slashed sections to it. Connect the topmost points of each slashed section to form a curved line. Trim the paper so that it is even with the new curve of the sleeve cap and attach it to the lower portion of the sleeve, matching the underarm points.

### SLEEVE FLARED BELOW THE CAP

You may follow the same steps to create flare just below the sleeve cap as you did to flare the sleeve cap for a leg-of-mutton sleeve, although you will generally need only five slash lines.

Straighten the sleeve pattern from the underarm points to the lower edge. Then, slash and spread the lower part of the sleeve, maintaining the position of the underarm points. Back the slashed sections with *Perky* Pattern Paper as previously described and attach the paper to the upper part of the sleeve pattern. (Fig. 52) Add ease to the back of the sleeve at the lower edge as described above for a long full sleeve with a fitted cap.

### BLOUSY SLEEVE

For a sleeve that is very full and blousy both at the wrist and through the cap, you should first slash and spread the sleeve cap as you did for a leg-of-mutton sleeve. Then, join the sleeve cap back to the lower part of the sleeve and retrace this new sleeve silhouette. After straightening the side seams, slash and spread the pattern as you would for a long full sleeve as described above. (Fig. 53) In this case, you won't need to remove the seam allowance from the cap before slashing and spreading. Add ease to the back of the sleeve at the lower edge if necessary.

## PUFFED SLEEVE

You may design a puffed sleeve by following the same procedure as you would use to add fullness to the sleeve cap for a leg-of-mutton sleeve, but make your adjustments on the short-sleeve version of the pattern. (Fig. 54)

## EXPANDED PUFFED SLEEVE

If you prefer to distribute fullness throughout a short sleeve, you will follow the same steps described for the blousy sleeve, using the short-sleeved version of the pattern for your alterations. A nice finish for this sleeve is elastic drawn through a turned-up casing.

You can begin to see the way designers use certain techniques to create new looks. With your basic Stretch & Sew Patterns, you can now do the same!

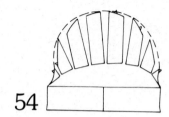

54

# 4

# Reversible Raglan Jacket
# Gored Skirt with a Wrap Panel

# Reversible Raglan Jacket
# Gored Skirt with a Wrap Panel

One of the most versatile of all Stretch & Sew pattern styles is the raglan sleeve top. Ranging in size to fit the smallest infant or the largest man, these patterns have an equally wide range of uses. A favorite is the reversible jacket with rib knit to trim the neck, cuff, and lower edge.

The raglan reversible jacket is excellent for learning the techniques to sew reversible garments. This jacket is not the only garment that can be handled in this fashion, although I feel the lack of a shoulder line does simplify construction. The techniques that you will learn are applicable to many Stretch & Sew Patterns. For instance, try the Tab Front Top with Cap Sleeves Pattern 250, the Cape Pattern 1010, or the Set-In Sleeve Jacket Pattern 1050.

To complement your reversible jacket, sew a skirt from the Stretch & Sew Gored Skirts Pattern 425 and add an extra panel to the front. This skirt will look like a wraparound and is quite sporty, especially with the addition of decorative buttons and topstitching. For an elegant look, make the skirt ankle length.

## Patterns for These Techniques

*Raglan Sleeve Top Pattern 200*
*Infants' Combination Pattern 850*
*Children's Raglan Sleeve Top Pattern 862*
*Raglan Sleeve Shirt Pattern 1710*
*Gored Skirts Pattern 425*
*Girls' Gored Skirts Pattern 867*

## Reversible Raglan Jacket
### Fabric

Because this jacket is usually an action garment, you will especially enjoy wearing it if you select fabric that is soft and comfortable. The fabric you select for one side of the jacket must be compatible with the fabric for the other side. The percent of stretch should be similar and the care instructions should not conflict. Before you cut out your jacket, be sure both fabrics have been thoroughly preshrunk.

There is a great range of fabrics you can use for this reversible jacket. Let your imagination be your guide and do some really creative things! I have seen some very attractive jackets made from cotton interlock — each side of the jacket made from a different color. Cotton double knits are lovely. You may wish to make one side from cotton single knit. Polyesters are great! Try a cotton terry with polyester and you'll have a terrific warm-up suit. Jacquard for one side and a solid-colored fabric for the other will add versatility to a jacket.

### Preparing Your Pattern

Because this jacket is to be worn over another garment, it is necessary to trace one size larger from your master raglan pattern than you would normally wear. For instance, if you would

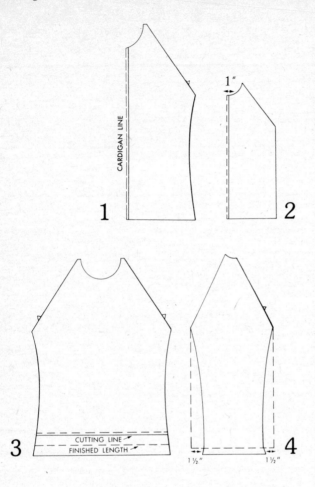

normally trace a size 34 for a knit top, trace a size 36 for your reversible jacket. If your fabric is especially firm, you will want to trace a pattern that is <u>two</u> sizes larger than what you would normally wear for a knit top.

Trace a back pattern piece from your master pattern. Then, trace a front pattern piece on the cardigan line. (Fig. 1) On children's and men's patterns, there is no cardigan line indicated, so you must add 1 inch to the center front to provide the cardigan lap. (Fig. 2)

Determine the finished length that you prefer for your jacket and subtract 2 inches from it for the width of rib trim that will be added. Then, add a 1/4-inch seam allowance and you will have your cutting line for the front and back. (Fig. 3)

To alter the sleeve pattern for the jacket, subtract the hem allowance but do not subtract the width of rib trim. This extra length will help give the slight blousiness necessary in a jacket sleeve. You will also want to add extra width. Extend the lower edge of the sleeve 1 to 1-1/2 inches horizontally on each side. Connect these points to the underarm and you will have your adjusted sleeve pattern. (Fig. 4)

## Cutting Your Fabric

Using your adjusted pattern, cut two complete sets of pieces from your coordinated fabrics.

For the jacket trim, you will need approximately 14 inches of rib knit. For the neck, cut a strip 3-1/2 to 4-1/2 inches wide by two-thirds the length of the neck, measuring on the seamline from center front to center front. For the cuffs, cut two strips of rib trim 4-1/2 inches wide. Each should be long enough to stretch comfortably over the hand plus 2 inches. For example, the trim for the cuffs should be approximately 7 to 8 inches long for a woman. The lower edge of the jacket will be finished with rib trim that measures approximately 4-1/2 inches wide by three-fourths the measurement around the jacket.

Cut two strips of *Perky Bond Plus* the length of the front and 1 inch wide.

## Sewing Your Garment

As you sew your jacket, remember to use 1/4-inch seam allowances unless otherwise specified.

On the wrong side of the fabric, apply one of the strips of *Perky Bond Plus* 1/8 inch from the front edge of one jacket set on each side. (Fig. 5) This will make a good stable base for the gripper snaps that you will use to close the front of the jacket.

Sew each jacket layer separately, joining the sleeves first to the back and then to the front pieces, but do not sew the underarm seams at this time. (Fig. 6) Press the seams toward the sleeves. A topstitching line 1/8 inch from the seam will also reinforce the stitching.

Fold the rib for the neck edge in half lengthwise with wrong sides together and divide the strip in four equal parts. (Fig. 7) Trim the corners from the cut edges to form a curve that stops at the first pin on either side. (Fig. 8)

Divide the neck edge of one of the jacket layers into four equal sections, measuring from center front line to center front line. With cut edges together, position the rib knit trim on the

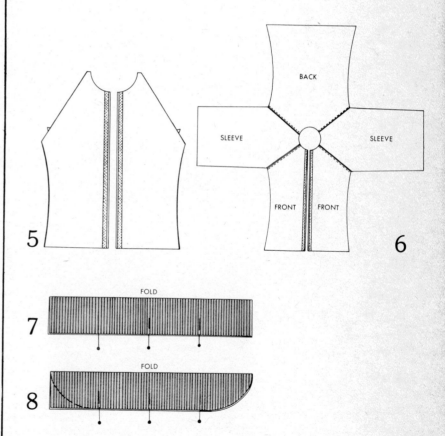

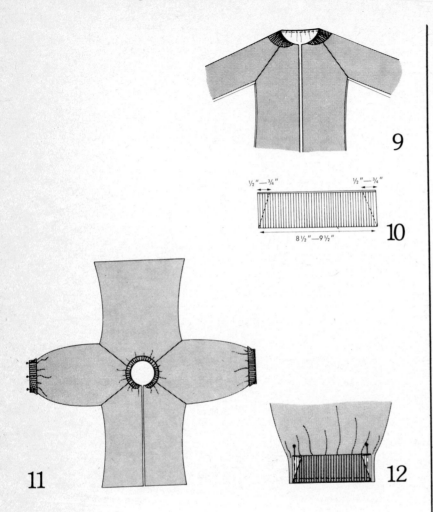

9

½"—¾"                                    ½"—¾"

10

8½"—9½"

11

12

right side of the jacket layer, matching the pins of the trim to those on the jacket. The curve of the rib will bring its folded edge to the neck edge of the jacket on each end. Sew the trim to the jacket, stretching it to fit the neck edge. (Fig. 9)

Take the two strips of rib trim that you have cut for the cuffs. With right sides together, fold them in half lengthwise and trim each end from the corner at the folded edge, tapering to a point approximately 1/2 to 3/4 inch in from the corner at the cut edge. (Fig. 10) The extra length on the folded edges will make it possible for you to lap the cuffs and finish them with a snap. Bond a 1-inch square of *Perky Bond Plus* at each end of the cuff strips to reinforce your snap closures. Stitch the ends of the cuffs and turn them to the right side.

Position one of the cuffs on the right side of a sleeve of one jacket layer and attach it with pins at the center and ends, allowing 1/4 inch of the jacket fabric to extend on each side. Stitch the cuff to the jacket layer, stretching the rib to match the sleeve edge. (Fig. 11) Pin the extending corners of the rib over onto the cuff so they will not be caught when you stitch the underarm seam. (Fig. 12) Attach the second cuff in the same way.

Now, with right sides together, place the second jacket layer along the neck edge of the first layer so that the trim will be sandwiched between them. Match the center back and all the seams of the two layers and sew along the entire neck edge over the previous stitching line.

With right sides together, pin the second jacket layer to the first layer at a sleeve edge, matching the center and each end. Sew across the previous stitching line. The first stitching will be quite gathered, having been drawn together by the cuff. So, stretch the first jacket layer and cuff to match the length of the second. Follow the same steps for the second sleeve.

Pin the sides and underarm seams of one jacket layer together. Then, stitch each side from the lower edge up through the sleeve seam to the cuff. Take care not to sew into the seam allowance at the cuff. Follow the same procedure for the second layer. (Fig. 13)

The lower edge is finished with a technique similar to the application of the neck trim and cuffs. With right sides together, fold the measured rib trim in half lengthwise. If you plan to apply snaps to the trim, bond a 2-inch square of *Perky Bond Plus* to each end of the strip for reinforcement. Stitch across each end (Fig. 14) and turn the strip to the right side.

Divide the rib trim into four equal parts. Then, divide the lower edge of one jacket layer into fourths, excluding a 1/4-inch seam allowance at each end. With right sides together, position the rib trim on the jacket layer, matching pins. Stitch, stretching the rib to match the length of the jacket's lower edge except for the 1/4-inch seam allowances.

With right sides together, place the second jacket layer on the first. Pin the lower edges together, matching seamlines. Then, sew over the previous stitching line, leaving 3 to 4 inches unsewn. (Fig. 15) Later, you will turn the jacket to the right side through this opening.

Complete the jacket fronts by stitching up from the lower edge on each side. Be careful not to catch the rib trim at the lower edge in this seam. Clip the corners of these seams. (Fig. 16) Then, press the seams open. This pressing will

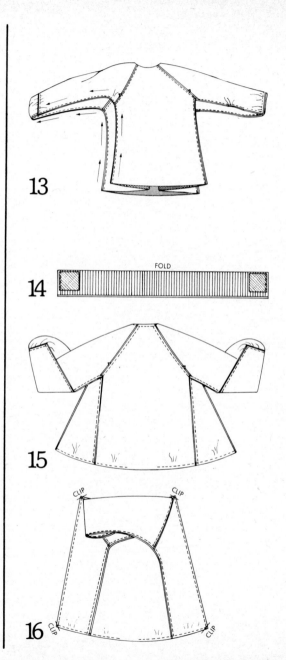

13

14

15

16

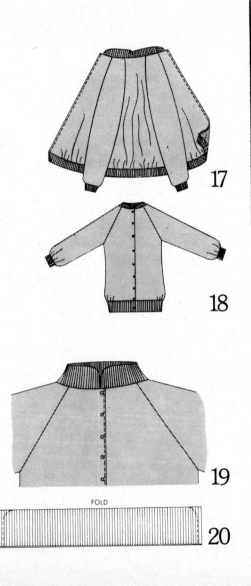

17

18

19

FOLD

20

help achieve a crisp finished appearance when you turn the jacket, so be sure to do it even if it seems awkward at this point in construction.

Turn the jacket to the right side by reaching into the opening at the lower edge. Grasp one sleeve edge and pull it out. Do the same for the second sleeve and then, carefully work the rest of the jacket through. A point turner will help bring the corners out nicely.

Position the layers evenly and press the jacket with care. Topstitch the jacket front edges 1/8 inch from the seam, sewing up from the lower edge. (Fig. 17) Turn the cut edges at the lower edge up into position and close the opening with a hand slipstitch.

Apply gripper snaps to the jacket front and to the cuffs, following the directions on the package. Amazingly, they will snap correctly whichever side of the jacket you wear out! Just apply them and see for yourself! This is such an enjoyable garment to make and even more fun to wear. Every member of your family will be eager for a reversible jacket. (Fig. 18)

## Variations

### MANDARIN COLLAR

For a jacket with a mandarin collar (Fig. 19), use the same length rib trim as you would for the neck trim on the jacket described above. A good width is 3-1/2 inches. Simply fold the trim lengthwise with right sides together and stitch across each end, forming a slight curve at the folded edge. (Fig. 20) Turn it to the right side and apply it to the neck edge of one jacket layer as previously described. This collar is also attractive if you use self-trim in place of rib trim. If you decide to use self-trim, apply it to the neck edge with a 1:1 ratio.

## TURNED-DOWN COLLAR

For a neck finish that will fold down (Fig. 21), cut rib knit trim 8 to 10 inches wide. Fold the trim lengthwise with right sides together and stitch across each end. Turn it to the right side and apply it with a 1:1 ratio to the neck edge of one jacket layer as previously described.

## UNRIBBED SLEEVES AND LOWER EDGE

For a less casual look to your jacket, you may want to eliminate the rib knit trim on the sleeves and at the lower edge. Cut your front and back pattern pieces at the desired finished length plus hem allowance. Then, construct the jacket in the same way, leaving out each step that requires sewing the rib to the sleeves or to the lower edge of the jacket.

The topstitching that goes down the front should continue around the lower edge of the jacket, and the sleeve edges should be topstitched as well. The opening at the lower edge which was used for turning will be closed with this topstitching, eliminating the need for any hand-stitching. (Fig. 22)

## ZIPPER CLOSURE

To apply a zipper in a reversible jacket with 2-inch finished rib at the lower edge, trace your front and back pattern pieces 1-1/2 inches shorter than the length of the teeth on the zipper you have selected. The jacket front should be cut with a 1/4-inch seam allowance beyond the center front line.

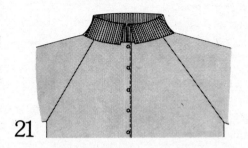

21

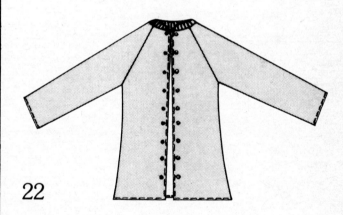

22

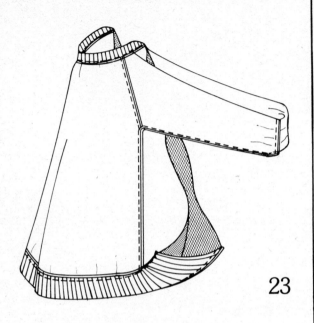

23

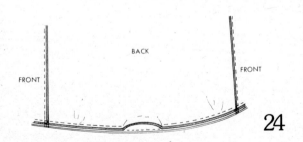

24

With one exception, you will assemble the jacket as described previously up to the application of the rib trim at the lower edge. When you apply the neck trim, allow the 1/4-inch seam allowance on the jacket front to extend on either side.

Divide the lower edge on one jacket layer and a single long edge of the rib trim into four equal divisions. Pin the trim to this jacket layer with right sides together, matching the divisions, and sew. Then divide the lower edge of the second jacket layer and the second long edge of rib trim in four equal divisions. Right sides together, place the rib trim on the jacket and stitch (Fig. 23), leaving 4 to 5 inches in the center unsewn for turning.

Separate the zipper and sandwich one section between the jacket layers. The tape should be placed even with the cut edges and the teeth should be toward the inside of the two layers, right sides together with the fabric that you will be wearing on the outside. The lower edge of the zipper should be 1/8 inch from the lower edge of the rib. Fold the zipper tape at the upper edge toward the cut edge of the center front.

Sew the center front edge, including the zipper tape in your stitching. Complete the second side of your jacket front in the same manner. When the jacket is turned to the right side, the zipper teeth will be exposed.

With the ribbing between the jacket layers, match the seam allowances and sew over the previous stitching lines. Start and stop the stitching about 1 inch from the zipper on either side, and leave the opening at the center back unsewn. (Fig. 24)

Turn the jacket to the right side through the opening and hand-stitch the opening closed. Topstitch the jacket 1/8 to 1/4 inch from the zipper teeth and it will be completed! (Fig. 25)

## NON-REVERSIBLE JACKET

For a non-reversible jacket, you must cut a facing pattern. Using your front pattern piece as a guide, draw a line that extends from the sleeve seam about 3-1/2 inches from the neck edge. Curve the line 3-1/2 inches from the cardigan lap and continue downward as illustrated. (Fig. 26) Cut two separate facing pieces from this pattern. Also, cut two pieces from *Perky Bond Plus*, trimming 3/8 inch from each edge. Bond the interfacings to your facings.

Sew the jacket together and add rib knit at the top and at the lower edge just as you would apply rib knit to the first layer on the reversible jacket. Then, with right sides together and the trim sandwiched between, stitch each facing to the jacket front, sewing over the previous stitching line at the lower edge. Take care not to catch the edges of the trim in your stitching. Pivot and continue sewing up the front. Pivot again and secure the facing at the neck edge by sewing over the previous stitching line. (Fig. 27)

Turn the facings to the inside and secure them by stitching-in-the-ditch on the sleeve seams. Apply gripper snaps or buttons and your jacket is done!

## NON-REVERSIBLE JACKET WITH A ZIPPER

To apply a zipper in a non-reversible jacket with 2-inch finished rib trim at the lower edge, trace your front and back pattern pieces 1-1/2 inches shorter than the length of the teeth on the zipper you have selected.

25

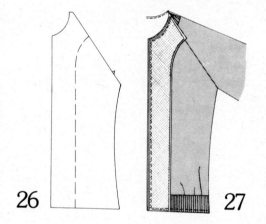

26   27

Draw a facing piece as described above and cut your facing and front pattern pieces 1/4 inch beyond the center front line. Construct the jacket up to the application of the rib trim at the lower edge, allowing the 1/4-inch seam allowance of the jacket to extend on either side at the center front when you apply the neck trim.

Divide the lower edge of the jacket and a single long edge of the rib trim into equal fourths. Stitch them, right sides together, matching quarter divisions. Then, with right sides together, position the lower edges of the facing pieces to the opposite long edges of the trim, keeping center front edges even. Stretch slightly as you sew.

Apply the zipper, sandwiching it between the facing pieces and the jacket front in the same manner as you sandwich a zipper between the two layers of the reversible jacket.

Quarter the unstitched portion of the second long edge of the rib trim and quarter the jacket between the edges of the facing pieces. Turn the trim up, matching the long edges with wrong sides together, and sew over the previous stitching line, stretching between quarter divisions. Then, turn the facings to the wrong side of the jacket and topstitch 1/8 to 1/4 inch from the zipper teeth.

# Gored Skirt with a Wrap Panel

## Fabric

This skirt is sporty-looking with its crisp lines, so fabrics with a fairly firm hand lend themselves more to the design than soft fabrics. Polyesters, acrylics, and many fabric blends are excellent.

You might enjoy making the front "wrap" panel from a contrasting or coordinating fabric. The combination might be used for a whole outfit. For example, you could make a reversible jacket to go with the skirt, using the same two fabrics.

## Cutting Your Fabric

The four-gored skirt design included with Pattern 425 is used as the basis for this skirt with a stitched-in wrap panel. Trace the pattern piece in your correct size and cut five and one-half gores from your fabric. Cut the half-gore as a facing for the left half of the wrap gore as you would wear it.

## Sewing Your Garment

Sew four gores together, leaving one seam unstitched. (Fig. 28) Then, press the seams open.

Prepare the wrap gore by sewing the facing to it, right sides together. The seam should be 5/8 inch wide down the side and the width of the hem allowance along the lower edge. (Fig. 29) Trim the hem allowance to 5/8 inch along the seam and clip the corner. (Fig. 30)

Turn the facing to the wrong side and press it carefully. Turn the remaining hem of the gore up into place and bond it with *Perky Bond*. Then, if you plan to topstitch the skirt, the wrap gore should be topstitched at this time. (Fig. 31)

Sew the wrap gore into the remaining seam of the skirt, keeping in mind that this gore has been hemmed and the rest of the skirt is unhemmed. The lower edge of the wrap gore should be pinned at the hemline of the skirt when you sew this seam. (Fig. 32)

Turn the hem up and bond it in place with *Perky Bond*. Then, if you are topstitching the hem, start at the topstitching line on the wrap gore and continue around the lower edge of the skirt, ending under the wrap gore at the seamline. (Fig. 33)

Use 3/4-inch Stretch & Sew elastic for the waist edge. Cut a strip of elastic that measures 1 inch less than your body waist measurement. Lap the ends 1/2 inch and sew them together to form a cylinder. Then, divide the elastic and the skirt waist into four equal parts and match the divisions, pinning the elastic to the wrong side of the skirt.

Stitch the elastic to the skirt along the upper edge — stretching the elastic to match the length of the skirt waist. A zigzag stitch is best because it has stretch, but a straight stitch may be used if you stretch both the elastic and the skirt as you sew. Finish the waist by turning the elastic to the inside and sewing again over the previous stitching line. An attractive decorative finish is to sew four buttons to the wrap gore as illustrated. (Fig. 34)

# Variations

### SKIRT WITH A ONE-INCH APPLIED WAISTBAND

To apply a waistband to this skirt, subtract 7/8 inch from the upper edge of the pattern. (Fig. 35) This will allow 5/8 inch above the waistline for the waistband seam allowance. Construct the skirt up to the waist finish, following the previous instructions.

For the waistband, cut a strip of fabric approximately 3-1/2 inches wide and 2 inches longer than your waist measurement plus two

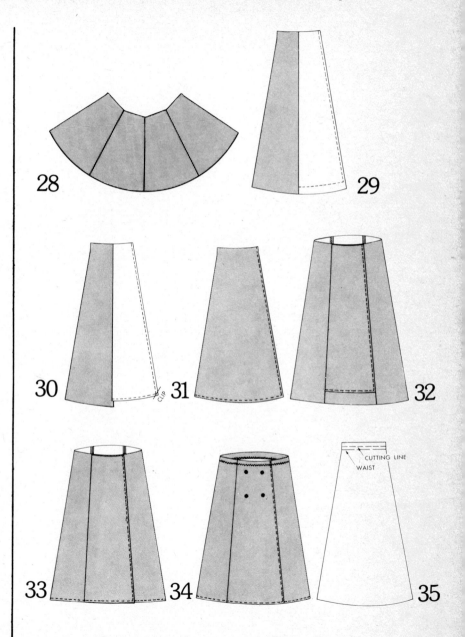

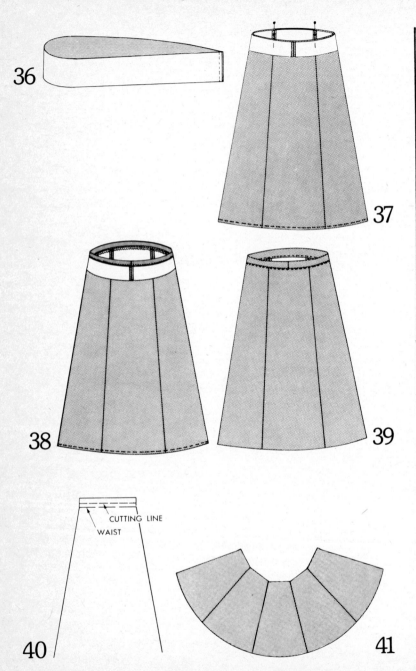

5/8-inch seam allowances. The stretch of the fabric must go the length of the strip.

With right sides together, stitch the short ends of the strip together. (Fig. 36) Divide the waistband casing into four equal parts so that the seam is midway between two pins. Pin the band, right sides together, to the skirt waist, matching the quarter divisions with the four skirt seams and placing the seam of the waistband at the center back. (Fig. 37) Stitch the band to the skirt with a 5/8-inch seam allowance and stretch hard as you sew.

Cut a piece of Stretch & Sew 1-inch waistband elastic as long as your waist measurement plus 1/2 inch. Lap the cut ends 1/2 inch and stitch them to secure the elastic in a cylinder. Divide the elastic in fourths and place it on the waistband seam allowance, matching the quarter divisions to the skirt seamlines.

Stitch the elastic to the seam allowance, using a zigzag stitch if it's available. (Fig. 38) If you use a straight stitch, stretch hard as you sew. Then, fold the waistband fabric firmly over the elastic to the inside of the skirt. Pin it in place and stitch-in-the-ditch from the right side. (Fig. 39)

## REVERSIBLE WRAPAROUND SKIRT

An attractive skirt that is simple to make is the reversible wraparound. This skirt requires an applied waistband. So, subtract 7/8 inch from the upper edge of the skirt pattern, leaving 5/8 inch above the waistline for the waistband seam allowance. (Fig. 40) Measure from the waistline for the desired skirt length and add 5/8 inch at the lower edge for seam allowance.

Cut five gores from each of your two contrasting or coordinating fabrics. Sew each skirt set together, leaving one seam open. (Fig. 41) Position one skirt layer on top of the other, right sides together, matching and pinning each seam in place. Sew the skirt layers together, leaving the waist edge open. (Fig. 42)

Clip the corners and press the seam allowances open for crisper edges when the skirt is turned. Turn the skirt to the right side and press it very carefully. Topstitch the edges to hold the layers in place. (Fig. 43)

For the waistband, cut a strip of fabric 3-1/2 inches wide. To determine the length, add your waist measurement plus one-fifth your waist measurement plus 1-1/2 inches plus two 5/8-inch seam allowances. For example, if your waist measures 25 inches, divide the 25 by 5 which is 5 inches. Add the 5 inches and the 1-1/2 inches to the 25 inches and the waistband length should be 31-1/2 inches plus seam allowances.

Divide the waistband, excluding seam allowances, and the skirt waist into four equal parts. Pin the right side of the the waistband to one side of the skirt so that the seam allowances at the ends of the waistband extend beyond the cut edges of the skirt. Stretching as you sew, stitch them together with a 5/8-inch seam allowance. (Fig. 44)

Cut a strip of Stretch & Sew 1-inch waistband elastic your exact waist measurement plus one-fifth more. For example, if your waist measures 25 inches, you will need a strip of elastic which is 30 inches long. Adding for seam allowances is unnecessary.

Divide the elastic in four equal parts and pin it between the waist seam allowances of the skirt, matching quarter divisions. Sew the elastic to the skirt, using a zigzag stitch if it is available. If you are using a straight stitch, stretch hard as you sew. (Fig. 45)

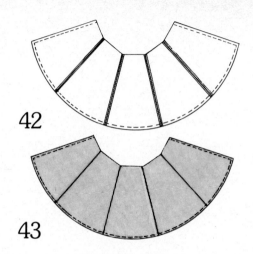

42

43

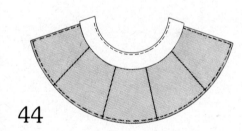

44

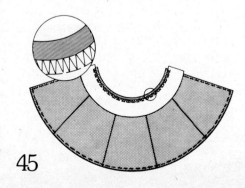

45

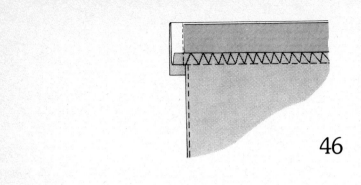

46

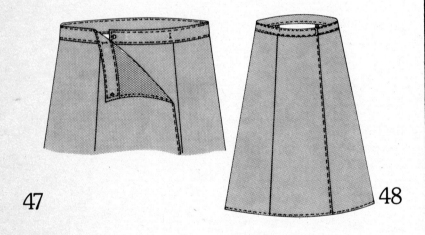

47

48

Fold the waistband the long way with right sides together so the fold of the fabric is even with the upper edge of the elastic. Sew the seam allowance at each end, taking care not to catch the elastic in the stitching. (Fig. 46) Fold the wasitband tightly over the elastic to the other side of the skirt and turn the cut edge under so that it just covers the original stitching line. Pin the band carefully in place and topstitch 1/8 inch from the fold. The topstitching line may be continued around the entire waistband for a decorative touch.

Sew two hook fasteners to the waistband by first placing the skirt in one of the ways it will be worn with the right side lapped over the left. Attach one hook underneath at the end of the right side and attach the second hook on top at the end of the left side. Stitch catches at the first gore line on each side of the skirt for the hooks to fasten into. (Fig. 47) To wear the skirt, simply lap the right side over the left and hook it into place. (Fig. 48) Even when the skirt is reversed, the hooks will be properly positioned.

## WRAP SKIRT WITH A FACING

For a wrap skirt with a facing, cut six gores from your fabric. Sew five gores together and use the sixth gore as a complete facing for the wrap gore. Sew the facing in the manner described for the gored skirt with a stitched-in wrap panel.

Cut and apply your elastic and waistband as described above for the reversible wrap skirt. The only difference is that you should place the elastic on the waistband side of the seam allowance. Hem your skirt with *Perky Bond* or with topstitching and you're done!

The basic patterns used in this chapter are delightful because of their versatility. You are bound to come up with unique combinations that will truly be "one-of-a-kind"!

# 5

# Cardigan Sweater
# with Round Neck
# Sweater Vest
# with Stretched-On V-Neck

# Cardigan Sweater with Round Neck Sweater Vest with Stretched-On V-Neck

Another reason for enjoying Stretch & Sew knit top patterns is that they lend themselves beautifully to garments made from sweater knits. A basic garment for any wardrobe is the sweater. On cool summer evenings or long winter days, both cardigan and pullover sweaters play an important role.

In this chapter I will share with you two classic sweater styles — a cardigan with a round neck and a pullover sweater vest with a stretched-on V-neck finish. Variations are included to add that extra incentive for creative flare.

## Patterns for These Techniques

*Set-In Sleeve Top and Sweater Pattern 300*
*Raglan Sleeve Top and Sweater Pattern 200*
*Infants' Combination Pattern 850*
*Children's Set-In Sleeve Top Pattern 861*
*Children's Raglan Sleeve Top Pattern 862*
*Raglan Sleeve Shirt Pattern 1710*
*Set-In Sleeve Tab Front Shirt Pattern 1750*

## General Fabric Selection

My first introduction to sewing with knits was with sweater knits back in 1965. The selection, for those days, was quite varied for us here in Oregon since the source of those lovely fabrics was the Jantzen Knitting Mills in Portland. In December, 1973, Stretch & Sew, Inc. established its own knitting mill. Within the first year of the mill's existence, the number of machines tripled — so we could increase the variety of stitches and patterns that we could knit for you, our customers, who had become as intrigued as I had long ago in sewing with these exciting fabrics.

Alpaca and wool yarn, knit in a beautiful links stitch, was our first exclusive Stretch & Sew fabric. This beautiful fabric has been granted the *Wool Mark* as a sign of its quality and performance. The all-wool links stitch does not ravel or run. It cuts easily and sews beautifully.

In the past, we instructed our customers to pre-block the alpaca all-wool links fabric, but today our knitting mill has a wonderful blocking machine so the fabric comes to you ready to cut and sew. Dry cleaning is necessary for the finished garment, but we recommend that you ask the cleaners not to press the garment. Over-pressing creates a flat, crushed appearance. A soft effect is the desired look, so pressing is not necessary. In fact, I recommend that with all sweater fabrics you should steam rather than press, rarely ever touching the iron to the fabric.

In addition to the all-wool links fabric, we also knit an acrylic links fabric. This is a good basic fabric for many home sewers. Because acrylic doesn't require dry cleaning, it is a very practical fabric for children's garments. Many people prefer to wear acrylic instead of wool, and this fabric has answered that need. The basic characteristics of the two fabrics are the same. The machine that knits the all-wool also knits the acrylic links stitch fabric. For the most part, garments are cut with the line of stitches (links line) running vertically in the garment.

We also knit a medium weight jersey, using acrylic. Rib trims are knit to be used with the jersey as well as with all of the types of sweater fabric that I have mentioned so far. With rib trims you may create a finished sweater look. Using matching yarns, our knitting mill also manufactures many types of flat and rolled-edge trims, making it possible for you to duplicate the ready-to-wear fashions you see in department stores and magazine advertisements.

And now we have jacquard sweater fabric made on double knit circular knitting machines which are intricate in their ability to produce fabrics that are unusual and beautiful. Many ideas for these sweater fabrics are brought to Eugene from the European markets that we visit twice yearly. Both Scandinavian and the more sophisticated French designs are seen in these jacquard patterns.

Because ribbed sweaters have become so popular, we have also developed ribbed fabrics which have been received with much enthusiasm. This sweater fabric has a finished edge to use in place of a hem.

All of these fabrics are dyed in colors to coordinate with the fabrics available in our Stretch & Sew Fabrics Centers so you can create outfits as lovely as any seen in ready-to-wear.

When it comes to fabric innovation, there seems to be no end to the creativity and ability of the designers of the world, and I can assure you that we will always be out there searching for the new looks in knit fabrics and making them available to you!

# Cardigan Sweater with Round Neck

## Fabric

For your cardigan, you will need sweater yardage plus rib trim for the lower edge. You will need rib trim specially knit with a finished edge for the cuffs and neck edge. A strip of flat or rolled-edge trim approximately 1-1/2 to 2 yards long is required for the finish at the front.

## Preparing Your Pattern

If you have chosen yardage with enough width, you may use the Set-In Sleeve Cardigan Pattern 620 which is cut without side seams. This is especially attractive with patterned fabric. You will need fabric 40 inches wide for the small size, 45 inches wide for the medium, and 48 inches wide for the large. The construction techniques described in this chapter work well with Pattern 620. You won't have to change the pattern, though you may wish to redesign the sleeves as described below.

I will use the Set-In Sleeve Top and Sweater Pattern 300 as an example in this chapter. The techniques will be the same if you prefer one of the other knit top patterns.

If you are using alpaca wool for your cardigan sweater, you should trace your pattern in your bust size. When you are using other sweater fabrics, check with your local Stretch & Sew Fabrics Center for specific information on sizing. Trace a front, a back, and a sleeve from your knit top pattern. Draw the front pattern piece on the cardigan line. This will provide the overlapping necessary at the center front for the buttons and buttonholes or snaps. (Fig. 1)

Determine the finished length that you prefer for your sweater and subtract from this measurement the amount of trim that you plan to add, leaving 1/4 inch for seam allowance. For example, if you want a 2-inch finished trim at the lower edge of your sweater, you will need to subtract 1-3/4 inches from your desired finished length. This will establish your cutting line at the lower edge of your front and back pattern pieces. (Fig. 2)

You must subtract some length from your sleeve pattern in order to allow for your rib cuff. Cut the pattern 1 inch above the hemline. Or, if you would prefer the sleeve to blouse down over the upper portion of the cuff, cut the pattern at the hemline. Now, extend the lower edge of your sleeve pattern 1 inch horizontally on each side and connect these points at the underarm. (Fig. 3)

## Cutting and Sewing Your Garment

Cut your sweater fabric from your newly adjusted pattern. Then, with right sides together, sew the shoulder seams of your sweater. The next step is to stretch in the sleeves. Match the center of the sleeve cap to the shoulder seam of the sweater, placing right sides together. Pin the sleeve at the shoulder seam and at each underarm point and sew, stretching slightly to keep both edges even. (Fig. 4) With right sides together, sew each underarm seam from the lower edge of the sweater to the sleeve edge. (Fig. 5)

For your fold-back cuff, you will need rib trim with a factory-finished edge. Cut two pieces approximately 4-1/2 inches wide by 6 to 8 inches long. Each one should be long enough to fit comfortably over the hand when folded in half

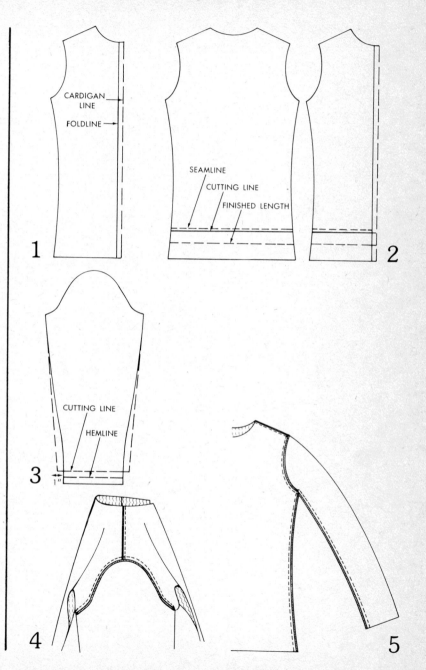

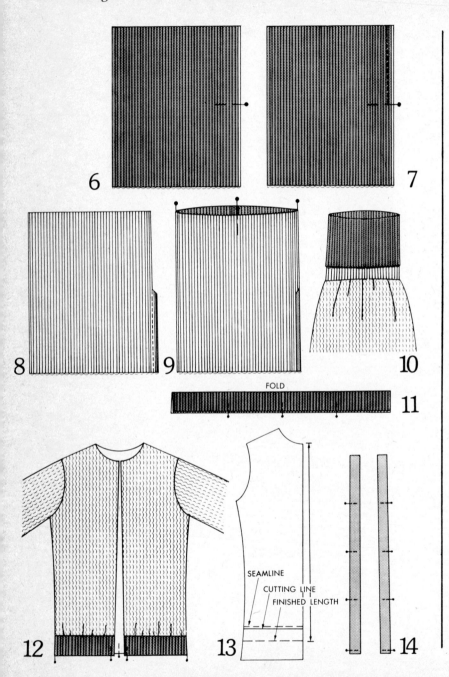

6

7

8   9

10

FOLD

11

SEAMLINE

CUTTING LINE

FINISHED LENGTH

12   13   14

lengthwise and formed into a cylinder plus about 1 inch. The rib lines on the trim should run parallel to the short ends of the cuff pieces.

Fold the trim in half, parallel to the rib lines and place a pin in the middle, fastening the two cut edges. (Fig. 6) Then, sew from one corner to the pin. (Fig. 7) Turn the cuff inside out and sew the remainder of the seam from the outside edge to meet the previous stitching line. (Fig. 8)

Finger-press the seams open and turn each cuff so that the seam allowance is inside at the end of the cuff with the unfinished edge. Divide the unfinished end of the cuff and the sleeve edge into four equal divisions. (Fig. 9) With right sides together, pin and stitch, stretching the ribbed cuff to match the sleeve edge. Fold back the ribbed cuff and it's finished! (Fig. 10)

The next step in constructing your sweater is to finish the lower edge with rib trim. Cut a strip of trim 4-1/2 inches wide (or twice the desired finished width plus 1/2 inch for seam allowances) by three-fourths the length of the sweater's lower edge. Fold the rib trim in half lengthwise and divide it into equal fourths. (Fig. 11) Quarter the lower edge of the sweater and pin the rib trim to the right side of the sweater, matching the divisions. (Fig. 12) Stitch, stretching the trim to match the sweater edge. Fold the trim down into position.

To finish the front, measure on your <u>pattern</u> piece the distance from the upper corner to the finished length line. (Fig. 13) Cut two strips of flat or rolled-edge trim this measurement plus 1/2 inch. Divide the sweater front into four equal parts. Then, divide the strips of trim into quarter divisions, leaving a 1/2-inch extension on each lower edge. (Fig. 14)

Lap the trim 1/2 inch over the front cut edge of the sweater on the right side, and pin it in place. The extra 1/2 inch at the end of the trim pieces should extend below the lower edge of the sweater. If you are using rolled-edge trim, place the roll against the sweater. Match the pin divisions and stitch from the lower to the upper edge on each side. (Fig. 15) Sew next to the roll on rolled-edge trim. For flat trim, the stitching line should be approximately 1/8 inch from the edge.

The extra 1/2 inch of trim should still extend past the lower edge of your sweater. (Fig. 16) Turn this extension to the inside. (Fig. 17) Then, fold the trim to the wrong side of the sweater and steam it lightly. The roll or flat edge of the trim will show on the right side of the sweater. (Fig. 18) Hand-stitch the trim at the lower edge to hold it in place. (Fig. 19) When you apply buttons and buttonholes or snaps, they will hold the remainder of the trim in position.

The next step is to finish the neck edge with rib trim that has one edge factory-finished. Cut a strip of trim 3 inches wide and two-thirds the length of the sweater neck opening plus 1 inch. You will want to measure the neck opening on the seamline which is 3/4 inch from the cut edge of the fabric.

Divide the cut edge of the trim into quarter divisions, allowing a 1/2-inch extension on each end. (Fig. 20) Now, divide the sweater neck edge into four equal parts. (Fig. 21) Pin the trim to the neck on the wrong side of the sweater, matching the quarter divisions. (Fig. 22) Stitch with a 3/4-inch seam allowance, stretching the trim from pin to pin to meet the neck edge.

Turn the trim up toward the neck opening. Then, fold it down with right sides together, with

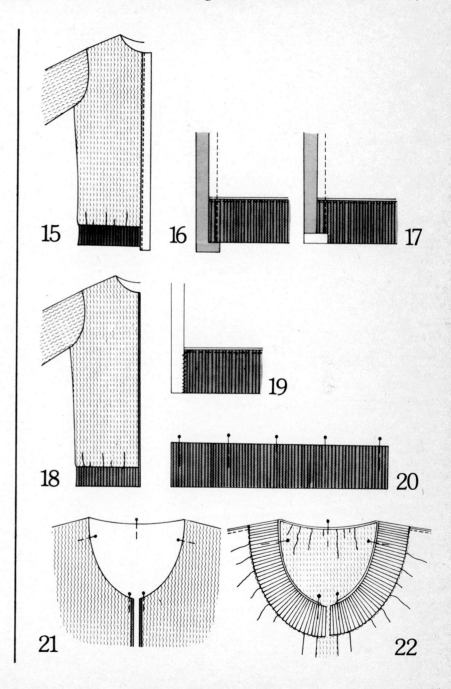

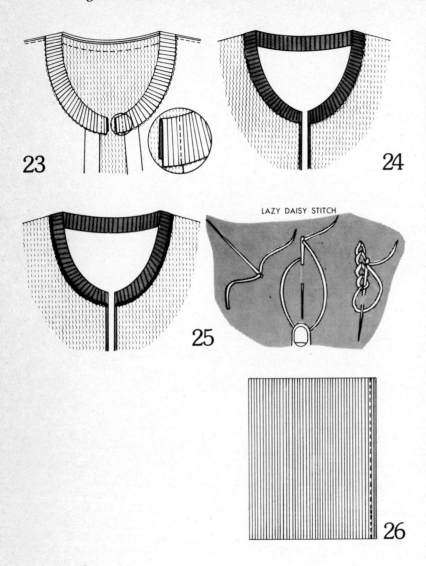

23

24

25

LAZY DAISY STITCH

26

the finished edge 1/4 inch below the seamline. Stitch across each end in a line even with the trim on the front opening. (Fig. 23) At the front edges where there is extra bulk, trim away the ribbing seam allowances.

Fold the trim over to the right side of the garment with the finished edge just covering the seamline. (Fig. 24) Topstitch the trim in place or, using a raveling from the rib trim, secure it with a Lazy Daisy embroidery stitch. (Fig. 25) Apply buttons and buttonholes or snaps to the front edge of your sweater. Buttonholes should be vertical except for the one in the neck trim which should be horizontal.

## CARDIGAN WITH SELF-TRIM

You might prefer to use your sweater fabric in place of rib knit trim on your sweater. Because self-trim does not have a factory-finished edge, the technique will be slightly different.

For the cuffs, cut two strips of self-trim 4-1/2 inches wide and long enough to stretch comfortably over the hand plus about 1 inch. The greater stretch of the fabric should go the length of the strip. Sew each cuff, right sides together, to form a cylinder. (Fig. 26) Finger-press the seam open and fold the cuff in half with wrong sides together. Divide the sleeve edge and the cuff in four equal parts. Pin them, with right sides together, and stitch, stretching the cuff to match the sleeve edge.

For the finish at the lower edge of the sweater, cut one strip of self-trim 4-1/2 inches wide (or twice the desired finished width plus 1/2 inch for seam allowances) and three-fourths the distance around the sweater. Apply this trim just as you apply rib trim. Then, continue with construction, applying rolled-edge trim to the cardigan front as described above.

For the neck edge, cut a strip of self-trim approximately 3-1/4 inches wide and three-fourths the length of the sweater neck edge plus 1 inch. You will want to measure the neck opening on the seamline which is 3/4 inch from the cut edge of the fabric.

Allowing 1/2 inch to extend on each end, divide the trim into quarters. (Fig. 27) Divide the sweater neck edge into four equal parts and pin the trim to the sweater with right sides together. (Fig. 28) Stitch, stretching the self-trim to match the neck edge.

Fold and stitch the ends as previously described for rib trim with a factory-finished edge. Grade the layers of trim at the front edges as described above. Then, turn the trim to the wrong side so that the cut edge of the trim is 1/4 inch over the seamline. Stitch-in-the-ditch from the right side to finish the neck trim.

## CARDIGAN WITH CONCEALED FLAT TRIM

A flat or rolled-edge trim is necessary on the front opening of your sweater in order to keep the edges stable. If you select flat trim and would prefer that its finished edge remain concealed, position the trim as previously described and stitch as close to the edge of the trim as possible. Then, the trim will turn completely to the inside of the garment.

## CARDIGAN FROM SWEATER BODIES

If you construct your cardigan from sweater bodies, the fabric will have a finished edge and it will be unnecessary for you to apply rib trim to the sleeve edges and to the lower edge of your sweater. Trace your front, back, and sleeve

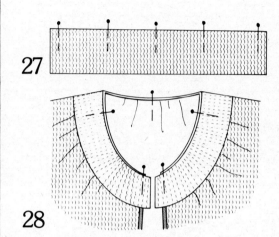

27

28

pattern pieces at the desired finished length. Generally, you will not need to add width to your sleeve pattern. However, if you plan to wear the cardigan over a long-sleeved garment, you may wish to add a small amount of width.

Cut your sweater with the lower edges of the front, back, and sleeves on the finished edge of the fabric. Construct the sweater as you would construct a cardigan from sweater yardage. Simply omit the steps in which you apply rib trim to the sleeves and lower edge.

# Sweater Vest with Stretched-On V-Neck

## Fabric

You will need the appropriate sweater yardage plus rib knit trim for finishing the neck, armscye, and lower edges.

## Preparing Your Pattern

Trace a front and back pattern piece from a set-in sleeve pattern. If you are using alpaca wool, you should trace the pattern in your bust size. When you are using other sweater fabrics, check with your local Stretch & Sew Fabrics Center for specific information on sizing.

Mark on the front and back pattern piece your desired finished length. Subtract from that length the width of trim that you will add minus 1/4 inch for seam allowance. For example, if you plan to add a 2-inch finished trim at the lower edge of your sweater, subtract 1-3/4 inches from your finished length to establish your cutting line.

Because this vest is to be finished sleeveless, it is important to straighten the underarm. (Fig. 29) Then, subtract from the armscye the width of trim that you plan to add. For example, if you plan to finish the armscye with 3/4-inch finished rib trim, cut 3/4 inch away from the pattern back and front at the armscye. (Fig. 30)

## Cutting and Sewing Your Garment

Cut a front and back, using your adjusted pattern. If you prefer a neck finish that will fall from your natural neckline rather than from slightly above it, trim 3/4 inch from the entire front and back neck edge. Then, fold your front in half, establishing a fold down the center front. Measure approximately 6 inches down this fold, depending on the depth of the V you would like, and cut from this point to the shoulder neck edge. (Fig. 31)

Sew the shoulder seams, right sides together. Then, for the neck finish, cut a strip of sweater rib knit trim 2 inches wide and approximately two-thirds the distance around the neck. (A little extra length is always wise.) Fold the trim in half lengthwise and position the raw edges along one side of the V, right sides together, allowing a 4-inch extension to finish the back neck edge. (Fig. 32)

Start sewing at the shoulder seam, going toward the point of the V. The trim should be stitched at a ratio of 2:3 (2 inches of trim to every 3 inches of neck edge) from the shoulder seam to within 1 inch of the point of the V. Gently pull the second side of the V down so that it forms a straight line with the first side of the V. Be careful not to stretch the fabric at the point of the V. Sew the trim to the sweater for 2 inches, stretching the trim very hard but keeping the sweater fabric relaxed. Continue stitching the trim to the second side of the V, using a ratio of 2:3 and stopping at the shoulder seam. (Fig. 33)

Measure the back neck edge of the sweater and determine two-thirds of this measurement. Each rib trim extension should be trimmed to 1/2 this length plus 1/4 inch for seam allowance. For example, if the back neck measurement is 9 inches, two-thirds of that would be 6 inches. Then, each trim extension should measure 3 inches plus the 1/4-inch seam allowance or 3-1/4 inches.

Open the ends of the trim and place them right sides together. Stitch with a 1/4-inch seam allowance. (Fig. 34) Finger-press the seam open and fold the trim in half again. Then, place the seam of the trim at the center back of the sweater neck edge. (Fig. 35) Stitch it in place, stretching the trim to match the neck edge.

From the wrong side, lightly steam the seam allowances and, pulling at the V, steam it to sharpen the point. It is easier to do this if you pin the shoulder seams to the ironing board cover.

After sewing the underarm seams, cut two strips of rib trim 2 inches wide and three-fourths the distance around the armscye. Sew the ends of each strip of ribbing together, forming a cylinder. Then, fold the trim in half lengthwise, wrong sides together. Divide the trim and the armscye into quarters, placing pins at each division point.

With right sides together, match the raw edges of the trim to the edge of the armscye at each quarter mark with the seam of the trim at the underarm. (Fig. 36) Sew them together, stretching the trim to match the armscye edge.

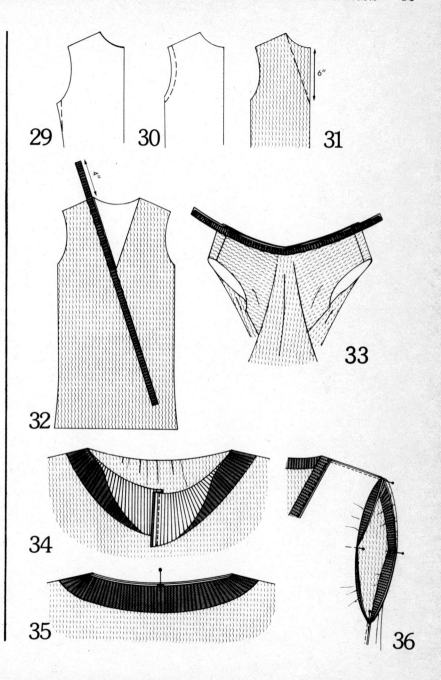

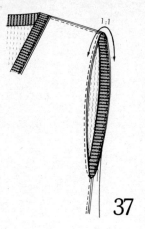

37

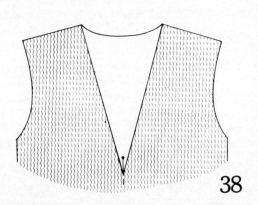

38

If you prefer a straighter line across the shoulder of your vest, pin the trim across the shoulder with a 1:1 ratio and stretch the remaining trim through the underarm. (Fig. 37) In this way, the trim won't be as snug over the shoulder.

For the finish at the lower edge of the sweater vest, cut a strip of rib knit trim 4-1/2 inches wide (or twice the desired finished width plus 1/4-inch seam allowances) by three-fourths the measurement around the vest. Sew the ends of the strip together and fold the trim in half lengthwise, wrong sides together. Quarter both the trim and the lower edge of the vest and sew with right sides together, matching quarter divisions.

Your sweater vest is complete!

## Variations

### MITERED V-NECK WITH RIB TRIM

In Chapter One you learned a technique for mitering a V-neck which is fun to do and can be used successfully with any fabric. Here is a second method which is simply done and very professional-looking, but which works most easily with ribbed knit sweater trim.

Adjust your pattern in the manner described for the vest with a stretched-on V. Because this technique provides a neckline finish that is 1-1/2 inches wide, trim 1 inch from the front and back neck edges before you cut the V on your sweater front as described for the vest with a stretched-on V.

Sew the shoulder seams. Then, cut a strip of rib knit sweater trim that is the measurement around the neck edge plus about 4 inches. The trim should be 4-1/2 to 5 inches wide. Place a pin on the sweater at the point of the V. (Fig. 38)

Position a single thickness of trim on the right side of the sweater so that the edge is even with the side of the V and 3 to 4 inches extend below the point of the V. (Fig. 39) Carefully insert the sewing machine needle so that the stitching will begin at the pin. Sew the trim to the neck edge, using a 1/4-inch seam allowance and a ratio of 3:4 on the sides of the V and 2:3 along the back neck edge. Continue around the neck edge until you reach the pin, making sure your stitching lines meet exactly at the point of the V. Hand-wheel the machine the last few stitches so that you do not damage your sewing machine needle by hitting the pin.

Turn the sweater vest to the wrong side and clip into the seam allowance to the point of the V, taking care not to clip into the stitching. (Fig. 40) Lightly steam or finger-press the seam allowance open.

Turn the trim up, bringing the ends of the trim to the wrong side. Then, fold the sweater on the center front with right sides together. Position a straight edge along the fold of the sweater so that it extends onto the rib trim. Locate the point on the trim where an imaginary line from the ruler perpendicular to the seamline is 1-1/2 inches long. (Fig. 41)

Backtacking about three stitches at the beginning and end, sew a line from this point in line with the center front fold of the sweater. This stitching should end at the point of the V. (Fig. 42)

Fold the trim to the wrong side and — as if by magic — you will find a completed miter on the inside as well as on the outside! Carefully steam any fullness from around the miter and pin the trim in place. (Fig. 43) It is crucial that you let

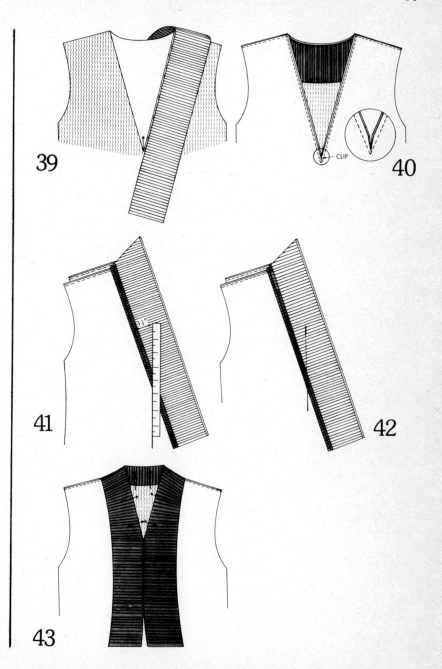

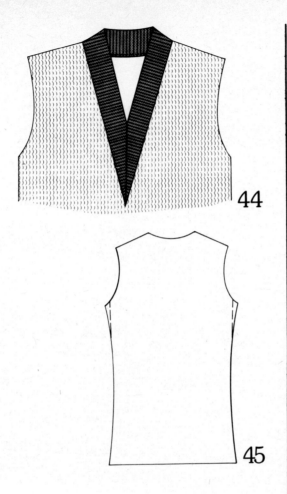

44

45

the sweater fabric cool before continuing so that it will not stretch while you are working with it.

To finish this neck edge, stitch-in-the-ditch from the right side. (Fig. 44) Or, fold back the garment on one side, exposing the seam allowance. Sew over the previous stitching line, including the trim in this stitching. Finish the other side and the back neck edge in the same manner.

Trim any excess rib 1/4 inch from the stitching line. If the fabric has a tendency to fray, sew a second row of straight stitching on the seam allowance 1/8 inch from the edge.

## SWEATER VEST WITH HEM AT ARMSCYE AND LOWER EDGE

For those who prefer a straighter line to the pullover sweater vest, it is simple to eliminate the trim from the armscye and lower edge.

On your pattern, determine the finished length that you prefer and add 1-1/2 inches for the hem. Straighten the underarm for a sleeveless finish (Fig. 45), but do not trim the armscye.

When you are sewing your vest, turn under the 1/4-inch seam allowance at the armscye and hand-stitch it in place with a raveling from the sweater rib knit. Hem the lower edge in the same way, using a 1-1/2 inch hem. The turned-under edge at the armscye may be topstitched, but be careful not to stretch it more than just slightly.

## SWEATER VEST FROM A SWEATER BODY

If you make your vest from a sweater body, you use the finished edge of the sweater body for the lower edge of your vest. Cut your front and back pattern piece at your desired finished length. When you cut the fabric, place the lower edge of the pattern piece on the finished edge of the sweater body. Then, simply sew your vest, omitting the step in which you apply trim to the lower edge.

## PULLOVER SWEATER WITH A V-NECK

If you would prefer to use one of the V-neck techniques in a pullover sweater with sleeves rather than in a vest, follow the instructions given for the vest except do not alter the pattern at the armscye. Adjust the sleeve pattern and add cuffs as described in this chapter for the cardigan sweater.

## CARDIGAN AND PULLOVER COMBINED IN ONE GARMENT

If you like the look of a sweater vest under your cardigan but would prefer not to have two separate garments, it is possible to combine the two.

Cut just the front of the sweater vest. The V should begin 2 inches back from the shoulder neck edge for a stretched-on V-neck finish or 3 inches back from the shoulder neck edge for a mitered V-neck finish. (Fig. 46) Shorten the vest front so that the finished length line will be slightly above the seamline for the rib trim at the lower edge of the cardigan. Then, sew the rib trim to the neck edge, following the procedure described for the V-neck finish you have selected. Sew rib knit to the lower edge with a 1:1 ratio. (Fig. 47)

Place the right side of the vest against the wrong side of the sweater fronts, matching the shoulder seams, the armscyes, and the side seams. Then, treat them as one piece as you sew them to the back of the cardigan. Now, you've achieved the two-in-one look!

So many garments can be created from fashionable sweater knits! Check your local Stretch & Sew Fabrics Center often for new ideas and sweater patterns.

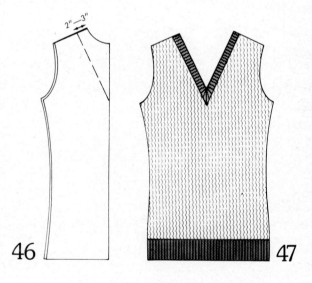

46   47

# 6

# Variations on the Shirtwaist Dress

# Variations on the Shirtwaist Dress

A classic design for any age is the Shirtwaist Dress, Stretch & Sew Pattern 1575. Shortened to blouse length, it becomes a sporty addition to a pants outfit or, extended to the floor, it's suddenly the perfect dress for a special evening.

The variations for the shirtwaist dress are as versatile as you wish them to be. In this chapter we will offer some suggestions and ideas that should get you going on another adventure in Stretch & Sew sewing. The shirt collar is a favorite of mine for many of my sportswear outfits. The innovation of the placket in the front of the dress has added a great deal to its interest and design.

You will also learn how to encase elastic at the waist and how to apply patch pockets with trim. Other variations will follow toward the end of the chapter. And, many of these ideas can be easily adapted to other Stretch & Sew Patterns!

## Patterns for These Techniques

*Shirtwaist Dress Pattern 1575*
*Body Blouse Pattern 790*
*Boy's Dress Shirt Pattern 930*
*Boy's Dress Shirt Pattern 935*
*Dress Shirt Pattern 1760*

## General Fabric Selection

Many fabrics can be used with great success for the shirtwaist dress. The fabric that you choose will determine the finished look of your dress — whether it will be soft and flowing or crisp and tailored. If you have a specific occasion in mind, consider the drape of the fabric to determine whether it will give you the look you want.

If you plan to use the same fabric for your entire shirtwaist dress, you will need the recommended yardage found on the pattern envelope plus one-half yard for the extra features you will be adding to the dress. If you plan to cut the collar, the facings with placket strips, and the pocket trim from contrasting fabric, you will need the recommended yardage for the main part of the dress plus one-half yard of your contrasting fabric. And, if you cut pieces from your contrasting fabric on the bias for special effect, you will need additional fabric beyond the one-half yard.

For the encased elastic at the waist, you will need a strip of Stretch & Sew 3/4-inch elastic at least as long as your waist measurement. A few extra inches is advisable.

## Preparing Your Pattern

Adjust your pattern to the length you desire and follow the pattern instructions for altering the bust dart to fit your figure. For more detailed instructions on altering the dart, refer to Chapter Three.

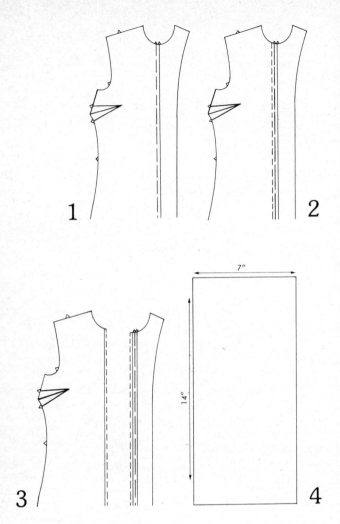

Measure your arm from the shoulder bone to the wrist bone and compare this measurement to the distance on the sleeve pattern from the cap to the lower edge minus seam allowances. If necessary, shorten or lengthen the sleeve at the lower edge before continuing. The cuff, when sewn to the sleeve edge, will push the sleeve up to provide fullness.

To prepare your pattern for separate facings with placket strips, carefully mark in the foldline and the center front line on your front pattern piece. (Fig. 1) Draw a third line toward the main part of the pattern front that is the same distance from the center front line as the center front line is from the foldline. (Fig. 2)

Cut on this third line, separating the facing from the rest of the pattern, and add a seam allowance to each cut edge. (Fig. 3) The portion which you have removed from the front pattern piece is your pattern piece for the facing with the placket strip.

Mark the buttonhole placement on your facing piece. If you plan to use the encased elastic waist finish described in this chapter, establish your own buttonhole positions, making sure that one is placed at the waistline.

For patch pockets with trim, cut a pattern that measures about 7 inches in width and 14 inches in length. (Fig. 4) This will give you a finished pocket that will measure approximately 6 inches square.

## Cutting Your Fabric

Cut the garment from your adjusted pattern. From your dress fabric, you will need one back, two fronts, two sleeves, two cuffs, two pockets, and, if desired, one belt 1 to 2 inches wider than the belt pattern piece. For the encased elastic waist finish, cut one strip of fabric, 1-1/8 inches wide by the length of the pattern measurement at the waist.

From contrasting fabric, cut one upper collar, one under collar, two facings with placket strips, and two strips, 1-5/8 inches by 7 inches, for pocket trim.

From *Perky Bond Plus,* cut one upper collar, two collar stands, two facings with placket strips and two cuff interfacings cut from the foldline to one edge of the cuff pattern.

To eliminate extra bulk, trim 3/8 inch away from each edge that will not be placed next to a foldline.

## Sewing Your Garment

The first step in constructing your shirtwaist dress is to bond each *Perky Bond Plus* piece to its companion garment piece. When bonding, place the adhesive side of *Perky Bond Plus* against the wrong side of the fabric and press, using a hot iron at the cotton setting. Protect the fabric with a damp cloth, pressing until the cloth is dry. Bond the upper half of each cuff piece. Bond one collar stand to the under collar and one collar stand to the upper collar after the entire collar piece has been bonded.

Continue with construction, remembering to use 5/8-inch seam allowances throughout unless otherwise specified. Stitch the darts and press them down. (Fig. 5) With right sides together, sew the facings with placket strips to the garment fronts. (Fig. 6)

For a raised appearance to the placket strips, the seam allowances should be pressed toward the

5

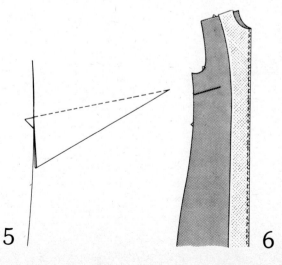

6

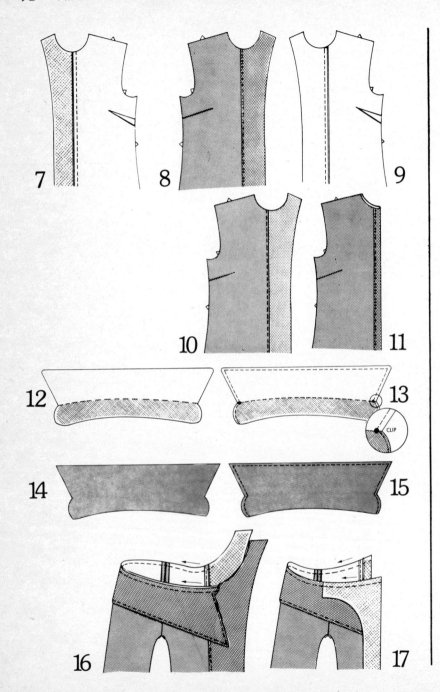

facings. (Fig. 7) Topstitch 1/4 inch toward the facing from the seamline. (Fig. 8) For a slightly inset look to the placket strips, press the seam allowances toward the garment (Fig. 9) and topstitch 1/4 inch toward the garment from the seamline. (Fig. 10) Turn the facing to the wrong side of the garment and press carefully to establish the original foldline as indicated on the pattern. (Fig. 11)

Sew the shoulder seams. On the under collar, stitch along the foldline, sewing on the edge of the *Perky Bond Plus.* (Fig. 12) Right sides together, sew the under collar to the upper collar along the outside edges. It is very important to stitch into the dots as they were drawn on the pattern. Trim the collar seam to 1/4 inch and the tab section seam to 1/8 inch. Clip into the seam allowance to the dots. (Fig. 13)

Turn the collar to the right side and press it carefully, rolling the seam slightly toward the under collar. (Fig. 14) Topstitch 1/4 inch from the finished edge of the collar. (Fig. 15)

Pin the collar to the neck edge with the under collar against the right side of the dress. Match the center backs and match the front collar edges to the foldlines on the dress front. Machine-baste the collar to the dress, starting at the front on each side and ending at the center back. (Fig. 16)

Fold the facings firmly back over the collar so that they are right sides together against the dress. On each side, sew over the previous stitching line through all thicknesses. Start at the front fold and overlap stitches where they meet at the center back. (Fig. 17)

Grade the seam allowances along the neck edge. Leave the facing seam allowances full width and leave the upper collar seam allowance along the back neck edge full width.

Turn the facings to their proper position and secure the facings at the shoulder seams. This can be done easily by stitching-in-the-ditch or, if you prefer, by hand-tacking the facings on the wrong side of the dress. Another easy method is to bond the facings to the dress at the shoulder seams with *Perky Bond.*

With a straight or zigzag stitch, sew the upper collar seam allowance to the back neck edge of the dress from shoulder seam to shoulder seam 3/8 inch from the original seam. Trim close to this stitching line. (Fig. 18)

Now, stitch the side seams and press them open.

For the pockets, fold the trim strips in half lengthwise with wrong sides together and press. (Fig. 19) Place the cut edges of one strip to the right side of one pocket edge and pin it in place as illustrated. (Fig. 20) Fold the lower edge of the pocket up to match the cut edges of the trim and pin it in place so that the trim is sandwiched between the two ends of the pocket. (Fig. 21) Stitch with a 5/8-inch seam allowance.

Turn each pocket to the right side and shift the trim down about 1-1/2 to 2 inches from the top to create a foldline on your pocket piece. This fold will be the upper edge of your pocket. Press it in very carefully and, also, press in a foldline at the lower edge of the pocket.

Turn the pockets to the wrong side and press the trim seam allowances. If you position the seam allowances toward the top of the pocket, the trim will turn down. (Fig. 22) If the seam allowances are pressed down, the trim will turn up toward the top of the pocket. (Fig. 23) Using the pressed folds as a guide, stitch both sides of

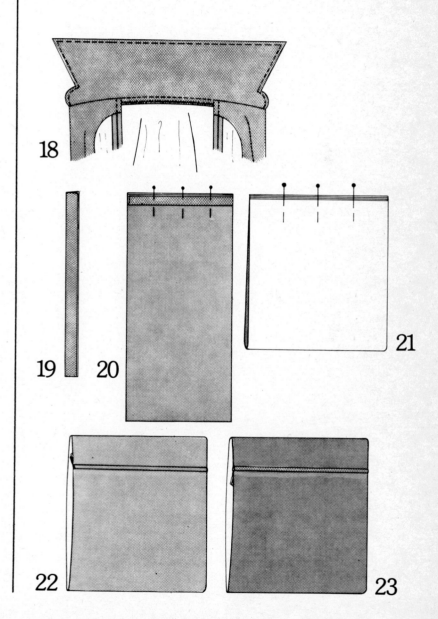

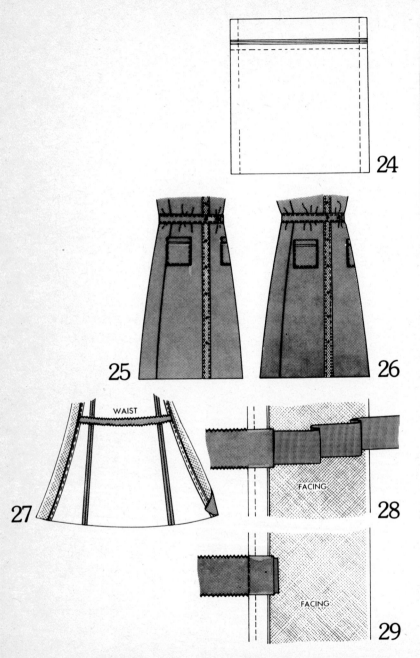

the pockets, leaving 1-1/2 inches open in the center of one seam for turning. (Fig. 24)

After turning the pockets to the right side, bond the openings shut with *Perky Bond.* Then, press the pockets again and topstitch them to the dress. On sizes 28 to 34, each pocket should be positioned approximately 3 to 4 inches below the waist and should extend about 1/2 to 1 inch over the side seam of the dress at the upper corner. (Fig. 25) On sizes 36 to 40, each pocket should be positioned approximately 4 to 5 inches below the waist and about 1/2 inch from the side seam at the upper corner. (Fig. 26)

To finish the waist with encased elastic, fold the facings out and position the 1-1/8 inch wide strip of fabric on the inside of the dress at the waistline. Each end should extend just beyond the placket seamline. Sew along each long edge of the strip with a straight stitch or with a small zigzag stitch. This stitching should end at the placket seamline. (Fig. 27)

Insert your elastic through the casing (Fig. 28) and adjust it for length. Generally, you should use a strip of elastic as long as your waist measurement. If your fabric is especially soft, the elastic may tend to pull at the center front closure. In that case, you should cut your elastic 2 to 3 inches longer than your waist measurement. If your fabric is firm and you prefer tighter elastic, you may shorten it a bit. After you have adjusted your elastic for the proper length, stitch-in-the-ditch along the placket strip seams to hold it in place. (Fig. 29) Trim away any excess casing fabric or elastic.

The long sleeve with a cuff is fun to sew and delightful to wear. Fold each sleeve along the slash with cut edges and right sides together.

Backtacking as you begin and end your stitching, sew along the upper end of the slash 1/4 inch from the cut edges. This stitching line should be about 3/4 inch long. (Fig. 30)

Sew the underarm seam on each sleeve. (Fig. 31) Then, press them open. Sew two rows of gathering stitches along the lower edges of the sleeves. Stitch the first row 3/4 inch from the cut edge and the second row 1/4 inch from the cut edge. (Fig. 32)

Sew the ends of the cuffs, right sides together, trim the seam to 3/8 inch, clip corners (Fig. 33), and turn the cuffs right side out. Press each cuff, rolling the seam slightly toward the underside. Topstitch 1/4 inch from the finished edges. (Fig. 34)

With right sides together, pin the cuffs to the sleeves. The cut edges should be even and the ends of the cuffs should be 5/8 inch from the edges of the slashes. Pull the bobbin threads to gather the sleeves to fit the cuffs. (Fig. 35) Then, fold the 5/8-inch seam allowances of the slashes firmly back over the cuffs and sew the cuffs in place. Remove the gathering stitches (Fig. 36) and turn the cuffs to the right side. Lightly press the seam allowances toward the sleeve. (Fig. 37)

Pin each sleeve into the armscye of the dress. The top sleeve notch should be positioned at the shoulder seam, and the other notches and the underarm seams should be matched. Sew in the sleeve, stretching the armscye to fit the sleeve. After you have checked the sleeve for fit, sew a second row of stitching on the seam allowance 1/8 inch from the first stitching line and trim the seam allowance to 1/4 inch. (Fig. 38) Now, lightly press the seam toward the sleeve.

For the hem, turn the front facings to the right side of the dress along the front foldlines.

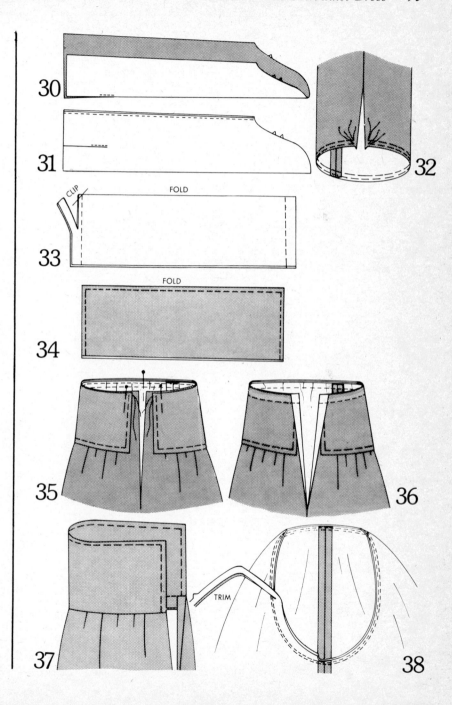

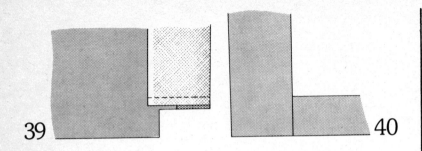

39

40

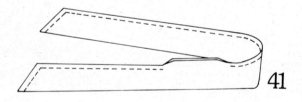

41

Then, stitch across the facings at the hemline. On each side, trim the facing and dress hem allowance below the stitching line as illustrated. (Fig. 39) Turn the facings back to the underside of the dress and press. Complete the hem with a hand catchstitch or by bonding. (Fig. 40)

At this point in construction, you may wish to topstitch the placket strips 1/4 inch from the foldlines.

Buttonholes on the cuffs and vertical buttonholes on the right front should be made according to the placement drawn on your pattern. Then, sew on your buttons.

The dress is very attractive with a belt or without. For a belt to be worn over the encased elastic waist finish, cut your belt 1 to 2 inches wider than the pattern piece. Fold the belt piece in half lengthwise with right sides together. Stitch from one end, starting at the fold and sewing diagonally to within 5/8 inch of the cut edges. Pivot and stitch along the seamline, leaving a 2-inch opening at the center for turning the belt to the right side. Complete the second end as you did the first. Trim the seam to 1/4 inch, leaving the 5/8-inch seam allowance at the opening. (Fig. 41) Turn the belt to the right side and press it. Finish the opening with hand-stitching or bond it closed with *Perky Bond.*

Now your dress is complete! It's a fun garment to sew and one that you will enjoy wearing for many occasions.

## Variations

### PATCH POCKET WITH A FLAP

For pockets with a flap, cut two pieces of fabric approximately 7-1/2 inches wide by 10 inches long for each pocket. Place the two pieces right sides together and stitch around all four sides, leaving 2 inches open for turning. (Fig. 42) Clip the corners, turn the pocket to the right side, and press. Bond the opening shut with *Perky Bond Plus.*

The upper 2 inches of the pocket will serve as the pocket flap. Topstitch, starting 2-1/2 inches from the upper corner, continuing across the upper edge of the pocket, and stitching 2-1/2 inches down the second side. (Fig. 43) Then, place the pocket on the dress and topstitch it in place, leaving the flap free. Turn the flap down and, if you like, sew a button to it for an added fashion touch. (Fig. 44)

## CURVED PATCH POCKET WITH TRIM

The patch pocket originally described can be adapted easily to harmonize with the curved line variation of the collar and cuffs to follow. After the seamline which sandwiches the trim has been sewn and the pocket has been pressed from the right side, turn the pocket to the wrong side and mark a curved stitching line at the lower corners, using a fashion ruler.

Stitch the sides and lower edge, leaving 1-1/2 inches on one side unstitched for turning. (Fig. 45) Trim the seam allowance to 1/4 inch and turn the pocket to the right side. Press it carefully and topstitch it to the dress. (Fig. 46)

For other patch pocket variations, refer to Chapter Two.

## CURVED COLLAR AND CUFFS WITH TRIM

Your dress will have an especially soft look with a curved collar and curved cuffs. Slightly round the corner on each collar piece with your fashion ruler. (Fig. 47) The curve on the upper

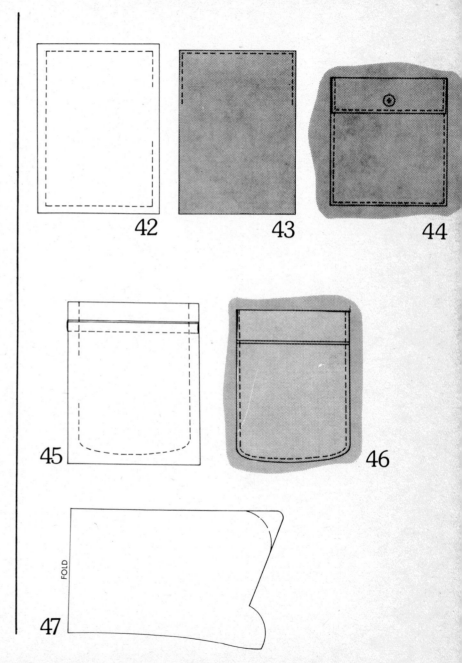

42    43    44

45    46

47

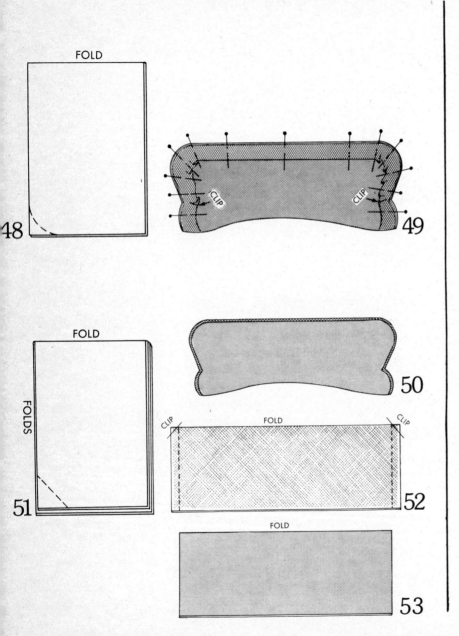

and under collar pieces should be identical. Cut the cuff along the foldline and add a 5/8-inch seam allowance along the cut edge. Curve the corners of the cuff as illustrated. (Fig. 48) Cut four cuff pieces from your fabric.

To apply trim to the collar for a piping effect, cut a strip of fabric 1-5/8 inches wide by the distance around the collar. The greater stretch of the fabric should run the length of the strip. Fold the strip in half lengthwise with wrong sides together and press.

With cut edges even, place the folded strip against the right side of one collar piece. Pin the strip in place and press carefully. Clip the seam allowance in the curves of the collar stand. (Fig. 49) Do not stretch the trim as you sew around the corners of the collar. Place the second collar piece right sides together with the first collar piece and sew over the previous stitching line. After you have sewn the seam, trim the straighter edges to 1/4 inch and the curved edges to 1/8 inch. Turn the collar right side out and press. (Fig. 50) Follow the same techniques to trim the cuffs.

## ANGULAR CUFFS

Fold the cuff piece and trim the corners as illustrated in Fig. 51. Construct the dress in the usual manner, pivoting as you stitch the angular corners on the cuffs.

## CUFFS WITH A FINISHED INNER EDGE

Fold each cuff in half lengthwise with right sides together and stitch the ends, beginning at the folded edge. Trim the seams to 3/8 inch and clip the corners. (Fig. 52) Turn the cuffs to the right side and press them carefully, rolling the seams slightly to the underside. (Fig. 53)

To apply each cuff, pin the upper half, right sides together, to a sleeve edge. Allow the slash seam allowance on the sleeve to extend at each end and gather the sleeve edge to fit the cuff. Fold the slash seam allowances to the inside of the sleeve and pin them in place. Stitch the cuff to the sleeve edge, leaving the under half of the cuff free. (Fig. 54)

With the sleeve right side out, place the right sides of the cuff together. Turn the cuff down toward the right side of the sleeve, exposing the cuff seam. On one side, wrap the unstitched edge of the cuff around the end of the cuff to the wrong side of the sleeve, so that the sleeve is sandwiched between. Matching the cut edges, pin this part of the seam in place (Fig. 55), and sew over the previous stitching line for 2 to 3 inches toward the center of the cuff. Grade the seam allowance to this point.

Repeat the same steps for the other side of the cuff, leaving at least 2 inches open in the center of the seam for turning. Turn the cuff to the right side and press the seam allowances toward the cuff. Bond the opening shut with *Perky Bond* or close it with a hand catchstitch. Then, remove the gathering threads and topstitch the cuff 1/4 inch from the outer edges. (Fig. 56)

## SHORT SLEEVE WITH A FAKE CUFF

For a short sleeve with a fake cuff, add 1/2 inch to the length of the short sleeve pattern. After sewing the underarm seam, fold the lower edge of the sleeve 1 inch to the wrong side and press. (Fig. 57) Fold it again 1 inch to the wrong side so that the cut edge is resting in the second fold. Press carefully. (Fig. 58)

Stitch 1/4 inch from the second foldline, making sure that the cut edge is caught in this

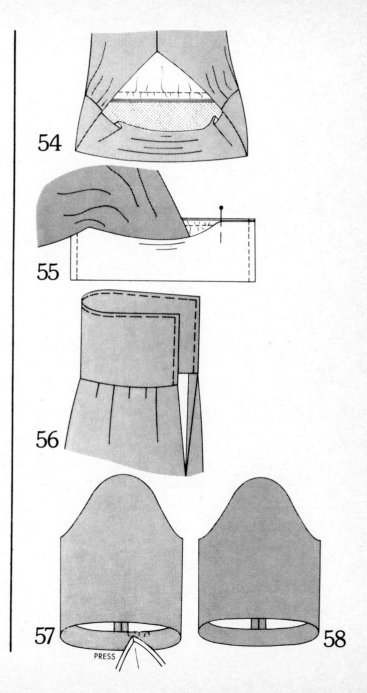

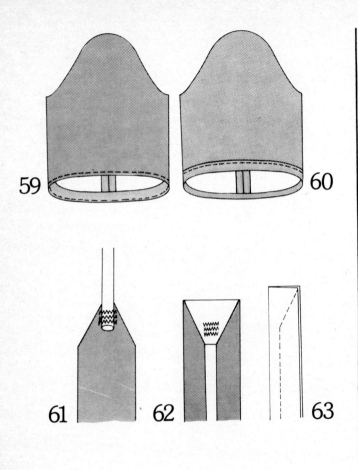

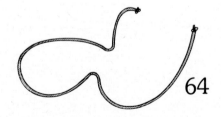

stitching. (Fig. 59) Turn the fold at the inside of the sleeve down, and press the fold next to the 1/4-inch seam toward the top of the sleeve and you have your "cuff." (Fig. 60)

## STRING TIE BELT

A nice variation for this dress is a string tie belt. Cut a strip of your knit fabric 2 inches wide and as long as you would like your belt to be plus 4 inches. This strip should be cut against the stretch. In other words, the greater stretch should go the width of the belt — not the length.

You will need a piece of strong cording longer than the belt piece to turn the belt to the right side after stitching. Cut a point at one end of the belt piece and stitch the cording to this end on the right side. (Fig. 61) Fold the point down toward the right side of the strip. (Fig. 62) Then, fold the strip in half lengthwise, right sides together, with the cording at the fold.

Start sewing at the end that has been turned to the inside, stitching from the cut edges toward the cord to avoid catching the wedge of the belt fabric which has been turned to the inside. (Fig. 63) Then, sew the length of the belt approximately 1/2 inch from the fold, stretching hard as you sew and taking care to avoid catching the cord in your stitching. It might be helpful to use a zipper foot.

Trim the seam back to 1/4 inch and turn the belt by pulling on the string. The point where the cord is stitched will start the fabric turning to the right side. After the belt has been turned, cut off the end where the cord was attached and tie a knot in each end to finish the belt. (Fig. 64)

## ENCASED ELASTIC BELT

For a belt made of elastic covered with self-fabric, use Stretch & Sew waistband elastic, which comes in 1, 1-1/2, or 2-inch widths. The length of the elastic should be 6 to 8 inches longer than the body waist measurement. Cut a strip of fabric three times the width of elastic plus 1/2 inch by the length of the elastic plus a 5/8-inch extension at each end.

Place the elastic on the wrong side of the belt piece, matching one long side. (Fig. 65) Stitch the elastic to the strip 1/4 inch from the edge. (Fig. 66) Fold the fabric over the unsewn edge of the elastic and turn the extension in firmly at each end. (Fig. 67) Fold the fabric over the elastic again, pin it in place, and topstitch around the entire belt 1/4 inch from the edge. (Fig. 68) On the wrong side of the belt, trim any extra fabric close to the topstitching line.

The belt laps 6 to 8 inches, right over left. A hook should be placed underneath at the right end and on top at the left end. Try the belt on to establish accurate positions for the catches. (Fig. 69) Buttons sewn to the right side will add a nice decorative touch. (Fig. 70)

So many fashions can be created from this basic pattern for the shirtwaist dress. Once you try the ideas in this chapter, you will be on your way to more fashion fun, sewing with knits!

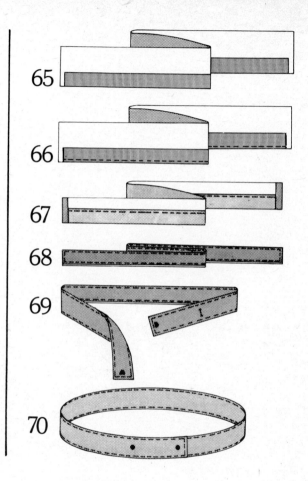

65
66
67
68
69
70

**7**

# Jacket with Double Chanel Trim
# Pleated Half-Circle Skirt

# Jacket with Double Chanel Trim
# Pleated Half-Circle Skirt

A Chanel-trimmed jacket would be a nice addition to any wardrobe. Because of its simple lines, Stretch & Sew Pattern 1050, the Set-In Sleeve Jacket, lends itself beautifully to this finish. This jacket is attractive as part of a pants suit or, when you wear it with the pleated half-circle skirt, you will have a lovely outfit for more formal occasions.

Applying double Chanel trim is a great technique and one that you will enjoy learning. I am sure there will be many times in your sewing future when you will be pleased that you understand this method. It is true that it is not as simple as making a T-shirt, but occasionally we find ourselves wanting a little more than the ordinary!

## Patterns for These Techniques

*Set-In Sleeve Jacket Pattern 1050*
*Ladies' Cape Pattern 1010*

## General Fabric Selection

Creativity has always been very important to me. I feel that as you develop skills, you will find the ability to create becoming easier for you. Do not hesitate to try many combinations in fabric. That is the great fun of being able to make the garment yourself.

There is just one important restriction. And that is the fabric care. The two fabrics which you select must be cared for in the same way. It would be possible to dry-clean polyester if you used it with 100 percent wool, but it is not a good idea to wash the wool. A blend of polyester and wool fibers in one fabric is often washable when the polyester content is greater than the wool. Just watch the combinations and be sure you will be able to treat both fabrics in the same way.

You will want to choose something that you will enjoy wearing for a while. Select a fabric that is classic in the sense that it will be as smart next season as it is this season. In my opinion, the time that you devote to this project calls for more than a one-season garment. When I was a young woman, my husband, Herb, did not always appreciate the value of my time. But I have always felt that it is very valuable to me and I think that many women share this feeling. (I might add that Herb's attitude has changed considerably!)

An example of a fabric with a perfect weight for this jacket would be *Miss Ann*™ polyester. As a guide in choosing other fabrics, select something that has similar characteristics. A balance in weight for the trim is a good choice. I have seen fabrics successfully used that are quite opposite in weight and hand, but you should avoid that with your first jacket.

A clever sewer will often find the reverse side of a jacquard double knit the perfect coordinate for the Chanel trim. For a bold look, try using

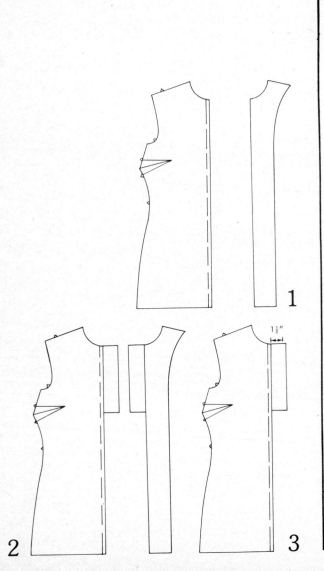

fun leather for the trim. A navy jacket with white trim is always a winner.

Or, you may combine fabrics with a subtle contrast for exciting results. Grey heather with white is an excellent choice. Try a tattersall check with a solid or the classic houndstooth with a solid. Pick up the solid in a skirt or pants to add interest and create an ensemble in which you will feel elegant.

As you can see, there is unlimited variety available to you in this Chanel-trimmed jacket, depending on your fabric selection. You will need the yardage recommended for your size on the pattern envelope plus 1/3 yard for the trim.

# Jacket with Double Chanel Trim

## Preparing Your Pattern

Trace all the pattern pieces in the proper size onto *Perky* Pattern Paper or *Do-Sew*, using the square collar for this Chanel-trimmed jacket. Adjust your dart for proper fit according to the pattern instructions. For more detailed instructions on altering the dart, refer to Chapter Three. Then, cut on the foldline of the jacket front pattern piece, separating the facing from the rest of the front. (Fig. 1)

In order to widen the lapel, cut two pieces of *Perky* Pattern Paper approximately 3 inches by 9 inches. Place one under the jacket front and one under the facing at the neck edge so that the length of the paper extends downward. (Fig. 2) Tape these strips securely in place.

Starting at the front foldline of the neck edge, draw a line 1-1/2 inches out. (Fig. 3) From this point, draw a line 1-1/2 inches straight down, parallel to the front foldline. Draw a slightly curved line to taper the lapel from the end of this line to the original edge of the pattern at the level of the bust dart. (Fig. 4) Draw an identical lapel on the facing (Fig. 5) and cut the extra paper away on each piece.

Cut 5/8 inch away from the upper edge of the extended lapel on your pattern front, stopping at the center front line. Trim the same amount from the facing. (Fig. 6) The untrimmed portion of the neck edge will provide seam allowance for applying the collar. From now on, I will refer to the jog in the pattern at the neck edge as the "collar notch."

Now it is time to mark the buttonhole placement along the center front line of your front pattern piece. You will transfer these marks to your right jacket front when you cut your fabric. The buttonholes are vertical and they will be formed as you apply the trim. The suggested buttonhole size for this jacket is 3/4 to 7/8 inch. (Select buttons the same size or slightly smaller than your buttonhole.)

The top buttonhole should be located just at the end of the lapel extension. The other button-holes should be equally spaced from the top one. There should be at least as much space between the last buttonhole and the hem as there is between buttonholes. (Fig. 7) If a button is placed too low, the jacket will appear unbalanced.

To adjust the square collar for the Chanel trim finish, cut the 5/8-inch seam allowance away from each end. (Fig. 8)

Allowing a 5/8-inch seam allowance at the upper edge, determine the desired finished length for your sleeve and cut the sleeve pattern piece at this length. (Fig. 9) The Chanel trim finish at the lower edge will neither add nor subtract from the

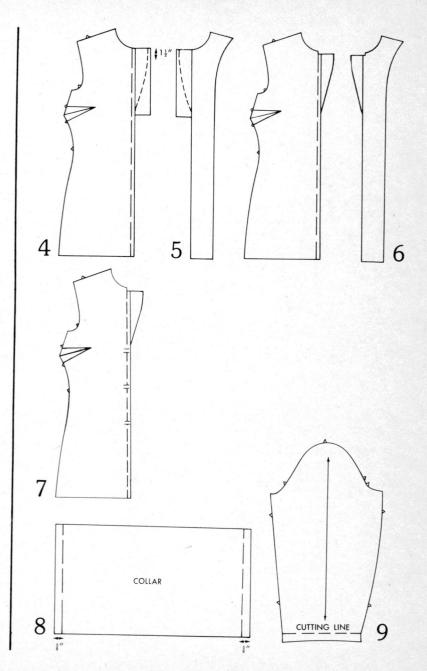

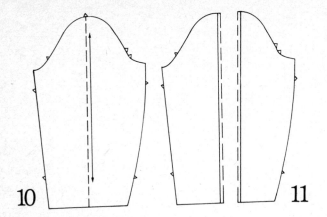

10　11

sleeve length. Draw a line straight down from the notch at the top of the sleeve cap parallel to the straight-of-grain line. (Fig. 10) Cut the pattern in half on this line. Then, add a 3/4-inch seam allowance to each cut edge. (Fig. 11)

## Cutting Your Fabric

Cut your fabric from the newly adjusted pattern. Then, cut *Perky Bond Plus* interfacing for half the collar and for the two facings. Trim 3/8 inch from all edges of the interfacing except those that will be placed next to foldlines.

For this jacket, cut strips of fabric that are exactly 3-1/8 inches wide for 3/4-inch Chanel trim. The strips must measure four times the finished width of the trim plus 1/8 inch. The extra 1/8 inch provides the necessary ease for double Chanel trim to fold over four thicknesses of fabric.

For the double Chanel trim on the jacket front, cut two strips that equal the length of the jacket front up to the corner of the lapel plus 2 to 3 inches. And, cut two strips as long as the distance between the lapel corner and the collar notch plus 2 to 3 inches.

For single Chanel trim on the collar, cut one strip that is as long as the finished edge of the collar plus 2 to 3 inches.

Each sleeve requires a strip for its single Chanel trim that is as long as the lower edge of the sleeve plus 8 to 9 inches. This will allow slightly more than enough but it is always better to have a little extra trim.

## Sewing Your Garment

Bond the *Perky Bond Plus* interfacings to the front facings and to the upper half of the collar.

As you apply the trim to your jacket, it will generally be easier if you stitch from the garment side. However, the illustrations for this chapter show the stitching from the trim side for the sake of showing clearly how the trim should be positioned.

With a flat sliver of hand soap, mark the four strips for the jacket front trim on the wrong side 3/4 inch from each edge. These will be your stitching lines. (Fig. 12) Match the lower edge of one of the long strips to the lower edge of your front pattern piece to mark the buttonhole placement on the strip. (Fig. 13) Use this strip for the trim on your <u>right</u> jacket front.

On the wrong side of both the fronts and the facings, mark 3/4 inch in from the inside cut edge, beginning at the collar notch, pivoting at the lapel corner, and continuing to the lower edge. (Fig. 14) Mark the buttonhole placement on your right front and right facing.

Stitching from the lower edge up, sew the strip for the left side to the <u>left</u> jacket front with right sides together. Stop 3/4 inch from the top of the lapel. (Fig. 15) In the same manner, stitch the shorter section of trim from the collar notch to the exact point where the stitching ends on the long section of trim at the lapel corner. Allow at least 1 inch of trim to extend at the beginning and end of your stitching. (Fig. 16)

With right sides together, sew the left facing to <u>the other side of the left trim</u> just as you stitched the left front to the left trim.

To prepare to sew the miter, draw a line to join the two corners of stitching. Mark the center point of this line and draw another line which extends up from the center point and is the same

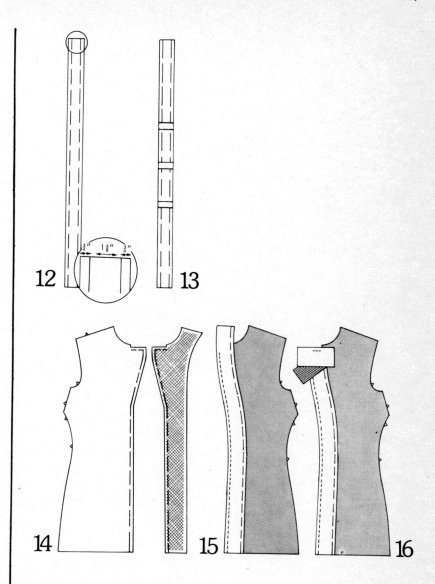

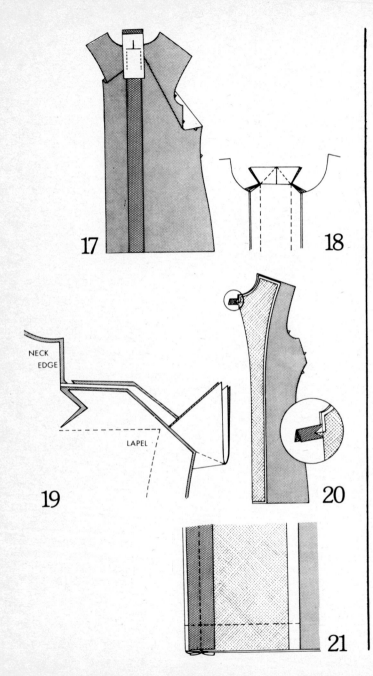

17

18

NECK
EDGE

LAPEL

19

20

21

length as the distance from the center point to one corner of the stitching. (Fig. 17)

Sew from one corner of stitching to the top of this second line. Then pivot and sew to your second corner of stitching. You will be sewing through a double thickness of trim only and the stitching will form an upside-down V. Cut away the excess fabric above your upside-down V.

Then, cut wedges from the trim so that your mitered trim will lie flat when it's turned. Cut the wedges as illustrated in Fig. 18, including the seam allowance of the jacket and facing in the lower half of each wedge. (Fig. 18)

Press the seam allowances open, using a damp press cloth so that they will stay in place. Turn the trim to its finished position and match the seamlines.

At the end of the trim by the collar notch, there is a bind created by the trim. At this point, clip wedges on the jacket front and on the facing seam allowances. Clip from the corner by the collar notch toward the lapel and then back to the end of the stitching. (Fig. 19) Fold back the jacket front and the facing, right sides together, and position the extending trim between the wedges. (Fig. 20) I prefer to baste this first and then to machine-stitch it. Cut the excess trim back to 1/2 inch.

To finish the lower edge, fold back the facing, right sides together with the jacket front. The inverted fold of trim should be at the edge and the seamlines should be matched. Stitch along the 2-inch hemline the width of the facing. (Fig. 21) Trim the facing hem allowance 1/2 inch from the stitching line. Cut away the hem allowance on the jacket front in the same way, stopping about 1/2 inch from the inside cut edge of the facing.

Follow the same steps to apply your trim to the right jacket front. The only difference is that you must skip the spaces you have allowed for the buttonholes, backtacking at the top and bottom of each one. (Fig. 22) You will also need to skip spaces for the .buttonholes as you stitch the trim to the facing.

To secure the trim on the jacket fronts, fold the facing back and sew over the previous stitching line, attaching the seam allowances of the jacket front and facing. (Fig. 23) It will not be necessary to sew the lower 3 inches or the upper 3 inches by the lapel corner.

This final stitching to secure the trim will finish one side of the buttonholes. The trim side of the buttonholes may be finished by hand-stitching although I rarely find this necessary.

Stitch the bust line darts and press them down. Then, sew the shoulder seams and press them open.

Fold the collar with wrong sides together and press it lightly. Mark your 3/4-inch stitching line on the outer edges of the under side of the collar. Then, mark the Chanel trim strip for the collar 3/4 inch from the cut edge on the wrong side of the fabric.

Right sides together, begin sewing the trim to the collar at the neck edge on one end. Stitch to within 3/4 inch from the corner and backtack. (Fig. 24) Remove the collar from the sewing machine in order to fold the trim to allow for the miter. Turn the trim back so that a fold is formed at a 45 degree angle to the corner. (Fig. 25) Then,

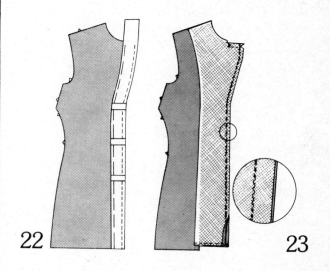

22    23

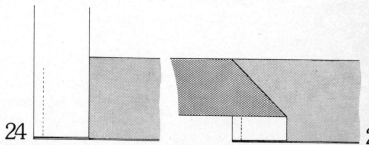

24    25

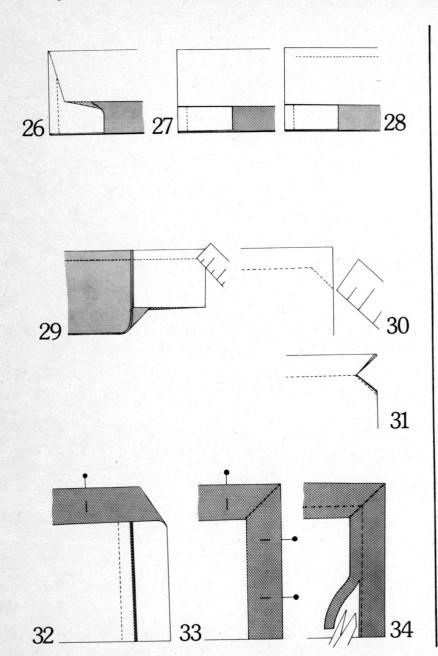

turn the trim again (Fig. 26) so that the cut edge of the trim and the edge of the collar are even and a second fold is formed parallel to the first line of stitching. (Fig. 27)

Starting at the exact point where the stitching stopped (Fig. 28), sew to the next corner, stopping 3/4 inch from the end. Fold the trim to allow for the miter in the previously described manner and continue sewing to the other neck edge.

To prepare to stitch the miter, place the collar so that the trim side is down. Fold the short end of the collar on the diagonal so that it lies flush with the folded edge of the collar. The wedge of trim will extend. Place a ruler on the trim with one corner against the pivot point of stitching and an edge against the fold of the collar that has been formed underneath the trim. (Fig. 29) This will form a guide as you pencil a line to get the correct 45 degree angle.

Sew on this line from the folded edge of the trim to the pivot point of stitching. (Fig. 30) Clip a wedge in the trim by cutting above this line of stitching to the pivot point and back to the corner of the collar. (Fig. 31) Sew the miter on the other collar corner, following the same procedures as for the first.

Turn the trim to the underside of the collar and pin it in place, starting at the center back and working toward the corners. (Fig. 32) Turn the trim at the ends to the underside and a miter will fold in place at each corner. Pin each miter carefully. (Fig. 33) Stitch-in-the-ditch from the right side to secure the trim and cut away the excess fabric close to the stitching line. (Fig. 34)

Pin the center of the collar to the center back of the jacket with the underside of the collar next to the right side of the jacket. Pin the collar edges to the center front of the jacket so that the trim of the collar is next to the trim of the lapel. (Fig. 35) Machine-baste the collar to the jacket from the center front to the center back on both the left and right sides.

Fold the facings firmly back over the collar so that they are right sides together against the jacket. On each side, sew over the previous stitching line through all thicknesses. Start at the front fold and overlap stitches where they meet at the center back. (Fig. 36)

Grade the seam allowances along the neck edge. Leave the facing seam allowances full width and leave the upper collar seam allowance along the back neck edge full width.

Turn the facings to their proper position and secure the facings at the shoulder seams. This can be done easily by stitching-in-the-ditch or, if you prefer by hand-tacking the facings on the wrong side of the jacket. Another easy method is to bond the facings to the shoulder seams with *Perky Bond.*

With a straight or zigzag stitch, sew the upper collar seam allowance to the back neck edge of the jacket from shoulder seam to shoulder seam 3/8 inch from the original seam. Trim close to this stitching line. (Fig. 37)

Sew the underarm seams of the jacket and press them open. Then, stitch the underarm seam of each sleeve and press it open. (Fig. 38) Sew the center seams with a 3/4-inch seam allowance, starting 5 inches up from the lower edge. (Fig. 39) From the wrong side, mark the 3/4-inch stitching line for the trim on your sleeves. Start at the top of the opening on the <u>front</u> side of the sleeve and continue around the lower edge.

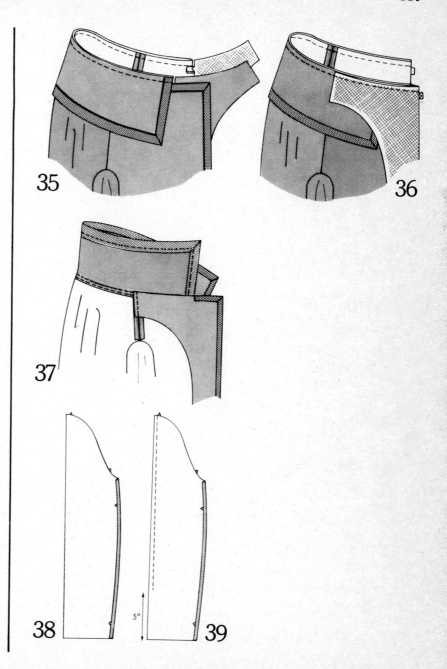

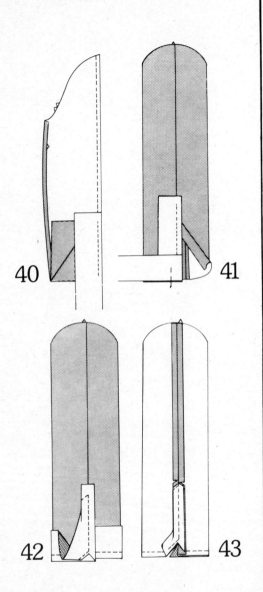

40  41

42  43

Mark the Chanel trim strips for the sleeves 3/4 inch from one cut edge on the wrong side. Position a strip of trim on the left-hand sleeve. The trim should be placed right sides together at the top of the sleeve opening on the side toward the <u>front</u> of the sleeve. One inch of trim should be allowed to extend above the sleeve opening.

Stitch from that point down, stopping 3/4 inch from the lower sleeve edge. (Fig. 40) Fold the trim for the miter as you did for the collar (Fig. 41) and continue stitching around the lower edge of the sleeve. Cut away any extra trim at the end of your stitching. Sew the miter at the corner on the front of the sleeve just as described for the collar.

To finish the overlap at the top of the sleeve slash, fold the trim, right sides together, and establish a fold 3/4 inch from the stitching line. Sew through the trim either up or down at a 45 degree angle from the folded edge of the trim to the initial point of stitching. (Fig. 42) Trim close to this stitching.

Then, match the fold of the trim to the cut edges of the seam allowances on the front of the sleeve opening. Using the stitching line at the upper edge of your sleeve trim as a guide, clip into the sleeve seam allowance to the initial point of stitching and cut away the trim seam allowance above this line. Clip straight into the sleeve seam allowance on the back of the sleeve opening 1/4 inch above your initial point of stitching. (Fig. 43) Now, press open the seam above your sleeve opening.

Turn the trim to the wrong side, folding the miter at the lower corner. Stitch-in-the-ditch to secure the trim and cut away the excess fabric close to the stitching line. The trim will lie on top of the unfinished side of the sleeve opening. Complete it by hand-tacking it in place or by sewing one to three buttons along the seamline through all thicknesses. (Fig. 44)

The finish for the other sleeve is applied in the same manner. However, it is done more easily if you start the first stitching of the trim along the lower edge of the sleeve and end at the top of the opening.

Set each sleeve into the jacket by pinning the upper seam of the sleeve to the shoulder seamline and matching the underarm seams. Sew, stretching the armscye of the jacket to fit the sleeve. When you are sure of the fit of the sleeve, sew a second row of stitching on the seam allowance 1/8 inch from the previous line of stitching. Then, trim the seam allowance to 1/4 inch. (Fig. 45)

Hem the jacket with a hand catchstitch or by bonding. Lightly press the completed jacket from the wrong side, using a press cloth. Don't press the roll line on the lapel, but steam it lightly at the point where the collar seam joins it.

Attach the buttons and your jacket is complete — an exciting sewing project and a joy to wear!

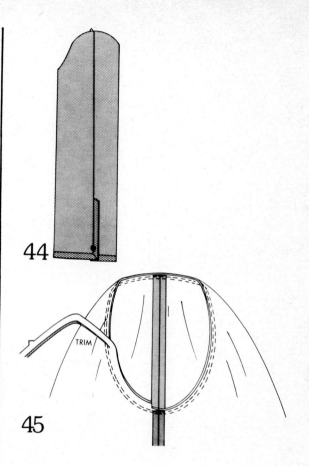

## Variations

### JACKET WITH SHORT SLEEVES

This jacket can be made with short rather than long sleeves. The only difference is the length of the sleeve's finished opening. Start the stitching on the sleeve seam 3 inches from the lower edge and you will have a jacket great for spring.

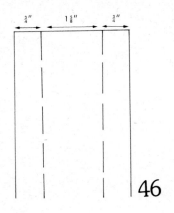

46

## JACKET WITH DOUBLE CHANEL-TRIMMED COLLAR

If you would prefer to have a collar with trim finished on both the upper and under sides, trim away the 5/8-inch seam allowance from each end of the collar as previously described for the single Chanel-trimmed collar. Then, after you have cut out the collar, cut it in half on the foldline.

You will need three strips of trim, each one exactly 3-1/8 inches wide. One should be the length of the long collar edge plus an extra inch or so, and two should be the length of the collar ends plus an extra inch. Mark the trim strips on the wrong side 3/4 inch from each edge. (Fig. 46) Also, mark the upper and under collars on the wrong side 3/4 inch from the ends and the outer edge.

Sew the long strip of trim, right sides together, to the long outer edge of the upper collar, starting and stopping the stitching 3/4 inch from the ends. In the same manner, sew the shorter sections of trim to the collar ends, stopping at the exact point where the stitching ends on the long strip of trim. With right sides together, sew the trim to the under collar just as you stitched it to the upper collar.

Sew each miter by first drawing a line to join the two corners of stitching. Mark the center point of this line and draw another line which extends up from the center point and is the same length as the distance from the center point to one corner of the stitching. Sew from one corner of stitching to the top of this second line. Then pivot and sew to your second corner of stitching. This stitching is through a double thickness of trim only and will look like an upside-down V. Cut away the excess trim above your upside-down V. (Fig. 47)

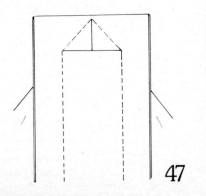

47

Then, cut wedges from the trim, including the seam allowances of the collar in the lower half of the wedges. To cut each wedge so that your mitered trim will lie flat when it's turned, clip from the upper corner of the trim to the corner of your stitching. Clip the second half of your wedge in a straight line with one side of your upside-down V. (Fig. 48)

### DOUBLE CHANEL-TRIMMED CAPE

You may apply the techniques you have learned in this chapter, using the Ladies' Cape Pattern 1010. Trace the square collar pattern piece from the Set-In Sleeve Jacket Pattern 1050 to use with your cape.

Follow the step-by-step instructions for altering your pattern and applying your trim as described previously for the jacket. The only exception is that you will need to trim 1/4 inch from each cut edge after you have separated your facing from the jacket front pattern piece on the foldline.

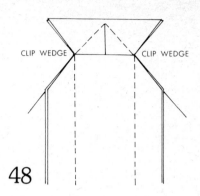

## Pleated Half-Circle Skirt

## Preparing Your Pattern

First, determine your waist measurement and subtract 1 inch. Divide this measurement by three to find the radius needed to draw the pattern. For example, if your waist measures 25 inches, you must first subtract 1 inch which gives you 24 inches. Divide 24 inches by three which gives you 8 inches. Eight inches is the radius that you would work with.

Add the radius you have determined plus your desired finished skirt length plus a 5/8-inch waist seam allowance plus 1 inch for hem

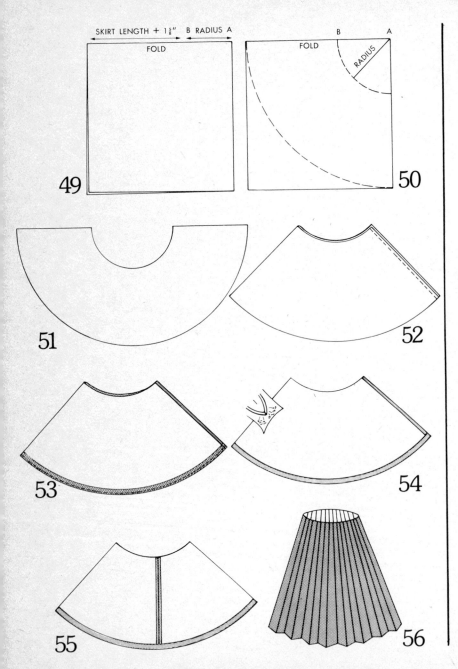

allowance. Cut a rectangle of *Perky* Pattern Paper or *Do-Sew* that is this length on the short side and twice this length on the long side. Fold this rectangle in half so that you have a square.

Designate one of the corners on the fold as point A. Measure along the square from point A the distance of your waist radius. This will be point B. (Fig. 49) Using a yardstick or tape measure and point A as your pivot point, draw a curve on the pattern for your waistline as illustrated. Again, using point A as a pivot point, draw the curve for the lower edge of your skirt pattern just as you did for your waistline. (Fig. 50) Cut on the two curved lines to get your skirt pattern. (Fig. 51)

# Cutting and Sewing Your Garment

Cut your skirt fabric from this pattern and with right sides together, sew the center back seam. (Fig. 52) Press the seam open.

Hem the lower edge of the skirt with a 1-inch hem. The easiest way to hem this skirt is to sew a strip of *Perky Bond* to the inside at the lower edge, stretching it slightly as you sew. (Fig. 53) It will pull the fabric up nicely to the inside and bond in place for a crisp finished edge.

With right sides together, fold the skirt in half at the center back seam and carefully press a crease on the opposite fold. (Fig. 54) Be sure that you use a damp press cloth and a hot iron to set these pleated creases. Match the crease to the seam and press the quarter divisions. (Fig. 55) Then, divide each quarter in half and press each eighth division. Finally, divide the eighth divisions and press in sixteenth divisions. Turn the skirt to the right side and press a crease between each inverted crease line. (Fig. 56)

Apply a waistband by cutting a strip of fabric approximately 3-1/2 inches wide and 2 inches longer than your waist measurement plus seam allowances. The fabric must be cut with the stretch going the length of the strip. Sew the two short ends, right sides together, forming a cylinder (Fig. 57), and divide the cylinder in equal fourths. Divide the skirt waist in fourths and, matching divisions, place the waistband right sides together against the skirt (Fig. 58) and sew with a 5/8-inch seam allowance.

Cut a strip of Stretch & Sew 1-inch waistband elastic your exact waist measurement plus 1/2 inch. Lap the ends of the elastic 1/2 inch and stitch. (Fig. 59) Divide the elastic and the waist seamline in equal quarters. Then, pin the elastic to the waist seam allowance next to the waistband. Stitch the elastic to the seam allowance with a zigzag stitch if available. (Fig. 60) If you use a straight stitch, stretch hard as you sew.

Fold the waistband fabric firmly over the elastic to the wrong side. Finish by stitching-in-the-ditch from the right side. (Fig. 61) Trim the extra fabric from the inside close to the stitching line.

# Variations

### HALF-CIRCLE SKIRT WITH A
### TURNED-DOWN ELASTIC WAIST FINISH

To use 3/4-inch elastic for a turned-down elastic waist finish on your half-circle skirt, substitute 1-1/2 inches for the 5/8-inch waistline seam allowance when you cut your pattern paper.

Cut a strip of elastic that measures 1 inch less than your body waist measurement. Lap the ends 1/2 inch and sew them together to form a

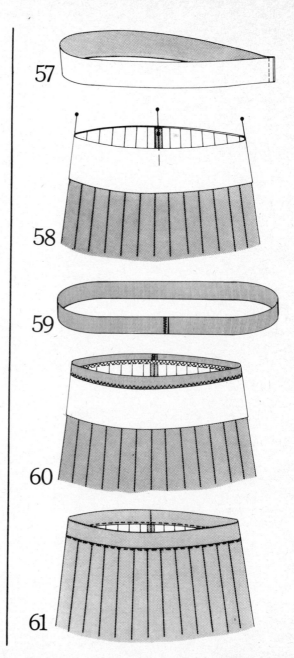

57

58

59

60

61

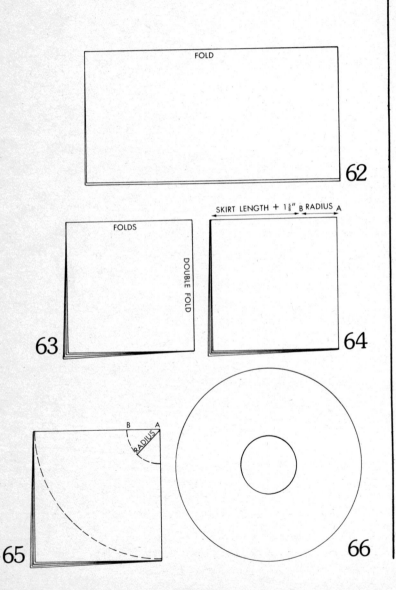

cylinder. Then, divide the elastic and the skirt waist into four equal parts and match the divisions, pinning the elastic to the wrong side of the skirt.

Stitch the elastic to the skirt along the upper edge — stretching the elastic to match the length of the skirt waist. A zigzag stitch is best because it has stretch, but a straight stitch may be used if you stretch both the elastic and the skirt as you sew. Finish the waist by turning the elastic to the inside and sewing again over the previous stitching line.

## FULL-CIRCLE SKIRT

To draw the pattern for a full-circle skirt, first determine your waist measurement and subtract 1 inch. Divide this measurement by six. For example, if your waist measurement is 25 inches, first subtract 1 inch, which leaves 24. Divide 24 by six which gives you 4 inches. This will be the radius you will need to draw your pattern.

Add the radius to your finished skirt length plus a 1-inch hem allowance plus a 5/8-inch waistline seam allowance. Multiply this number by two and cut a square piece of *Perky* Pattern Paper or *Do-Sew* which is this long on each side. Fold the pattern material in half (Fig. 62) and fold it again the other way. (Fig. 63)

Mark point A on the corner with the double fold and measure from point A along one edge the distance of your radius to find point B. (Fig. 64) Mark the curve for the waistline as described for the half-circle skirt. Draw a curved line for the lower edge of your skirt pattern, using point A as a pivot point. (Fig. 65) Cut on the curved lines and unfold the pattern paper for your finished circle skirt pattern. (Fig. 66)

Finish the skirt as previously described for the pleated half-circle skirt, except double the number of pleats. Or, you may omit the pleats if you prefer.

## QUARTER-CIRCLE SKIRT

For a quarter-circle skirt, subtract 1 inch from your waist measurement and multiply by two-thirds to determine the radius. For example, if your waist measurement is 25 inches, subtract 1 inch to get 24 inches. Multiply this by two-thirds and your radius would be 16 inches.

To draw the pattern, cut a square of *Perky* Pattern Paper or *Do-Sew* with each side measuring the radius plus the finished skirt length plus a 5/8-inch waist seam allowance plus a 1-inch hem allowance.

Designate one corner as point A and measure from point A along one edge the distance of your radius to find point B. (Fig. 67) Draw the waistline as described for the half-circle skirt. Then, draw a curved line for the lower edge of your skirt pattern, using point A as a pivot point. (Fig. 68) Cut on the curved lines for your quarter-circle skirt pattern.

Construct the skirt as described for the half-circle skirt, omitting the pleats because there is not enough fullness in this skirt for the pleats to hang freely.

You will have added a beautifully-tailored jacket and skirt to your wardrobe by following these step-by-step instructions. You will be eager to try it again on another outfit for yourself, or perhaps, for another member of the family.

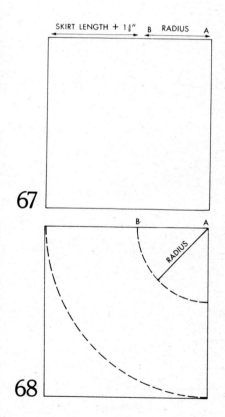

**8**

# Tank Swimsuit with Gathered Front and Circle Opening Hooded Swim Cover-Up

# Tank Swimsuit with Gathered Front and Circle Opening Hooded Swim Cover-Up

Many women need several swimsuits each summer. The classic tank swimsuit described in this chapter is a favorite for summer recreation. For years we have heard from our customers that they need a tank suit. This darted swimsuit serves not only as a racing suit but allows a new ground for creativity. The variations possible will give you the freedom to design to your heart's content.

Don't stop at a swimsuit. Sew a matching cover-up from one of the coordinated Antron* nylon prints or from a thirsty cotton knit to complete your outfit for sun-time fun!

## Patterns for These Techniques

*Tank Suit Pattern 1320*
*Set-In Sleeve Top and Sweater Pattern 300*
*Raglan Sleeve Top and Sweater Pattern 200*
*Children's Set-In Sleeve Top Pattern 861*
*Children's Raglan Sleeve Top Pattern 862*

# Tank Swimsuit with Gathered Front and Circle Opening

## General Fabric Selection

Stretch & Sew has the ability to design a pattern for a specific fabric — just like manufacturers. A pattern may be designed for one particular fabric and that fabric is the only one that is used with that pattern. Not all Stretch &

Sew Patterns are designed in this way. However, the Tank Suit Pattern 1320 is such a pattern.

This suit was designed for a warp knit of Antron* nylon and Lycra*. The finish of this fabric is varied. It sometimes has a satin finish. I have seen it brushed for a napped effect, and a mat finish has been developed. So, the finish is not a limiting factor — the stretch is the determining factor.

The primary stretch in this fabric is vertical and there is at least 50 percent crosswise stretch. The pattern is laid out to allow the most stretch to run across the garment. One yard will make most sizes.

## Preparing Your Pattern

Trace a personal pattern from your master pattern in your correct bust size. Then, find your overall body measurement by placing the end of the tape measure between the bones at the natural neckline in front. Bring the tape through the crotch and up to the prominent bone in the back at the natural neckline. (Fig. 1)

Compare your overall body measurement to the chart below:

| Suit Size | Overall Body Measurement |
|---|---|
| 30-32 | 54 inches |
| 34-36 | 56 inches |
| 38-40 | 58 inches |

*DuPont registered trademarks.

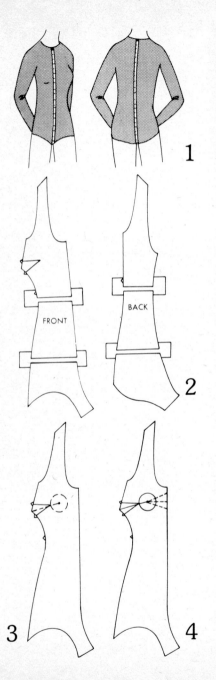

If your measurement does not coincide with the one on the chart for your size, you will need to make a body length adjustment, using the lines for shortening and lengthening on the pattern. Divide the amount of difference by four and add or subtract that amount at each line for shortening or lengthening.

For example, if your overall body measurement is 58 inches and you are making a size 36 suit, you need 2 extra inches in total body length. Two inches divided by 4 is 1/2 inch. So, in this case, you will need to add 1/2 inch between each line for shortening or lengthening. Separate your traced pattern pieces on these lines and place *Perky* Pattern Paper behind each division. Provide exactly 1/2 inch between the pattern sections and tape them carefully in place. (Fig. 2) Trim the pattern paper even with the outside lines of your pattern pieces.

If it is necessary for you to shorten the pattern, cut on the lines for shortening and lengthening and lap the pattern the appropriate amount.

In order to relocate your dart to gathers, draw a line through the center of the dart and extend it 1-1/2 inches beyond the point of the dart. The end of this line will be the pivot point for relocating the dart to gathers. Draw a circle around this point with a 1-1/2 inch radius. (Fig. 3) Because of the great stretch of the fabric and the fit of this suit, the 1-1/2 inch radius is appropriate for all women's sizes.

Draw three slash lines from the center front to the pivot point. The first line should extend straight across to the pivot point. The second line should extend from a point 1 inch above the first and the third line should extend from a point 1 inch below the first. (Fig. 4)

Cut on each of the three slash lines to the pivot point and, also, cut on the center line of the dart to the pivot point. Close the dart by pivoting the paper at the pivot point, bringing the notches at the end of the dart together. (The legs of the dart will not match along their entire length.) This will automatically open the slashed section at the front.

Place *Perky* Pattern Paper behind your pattern and arrange the slashed section so that the distance between each slash is equal. (Fig. 5) Tape the sections to the paper to stabilize them. Then, using your fashion ruler, draw a curved line which connects the outside points of the slashed sections. Trim away the extra paper.

To cut the circle from the center front, measure 2-1/2 inches below the lowest slash point. (Fig. 6) This will be the center of the circle. Using it as a pivot point, draw a circle with a 2-inch radius and cut the circle from the pattern. The edge of the circle will be 1/2 inch from the lowest slash point.

Your pattern is now ready to use. Isn't it fun to create your own design!

## Cutting and Sewing Your Garment

Using your altered pattern, cut two fronts and two backs from your fabric. Cut a crotch piece from swimsuit lining fabric or use self-fabric for the lining.

Sew two rows of machine gathering stitches on the front sections, starting 1 inch below the center front neck edge and ending 1/2 inch above the circle cut-out. One row should be 1/8 inch from the cut edge and the second should be 3/8 inch from the cut edge. (Fig. 7) Pull the bobbin

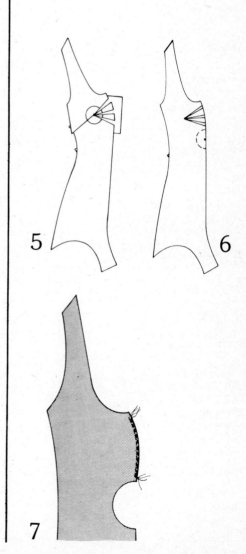

5   6

7

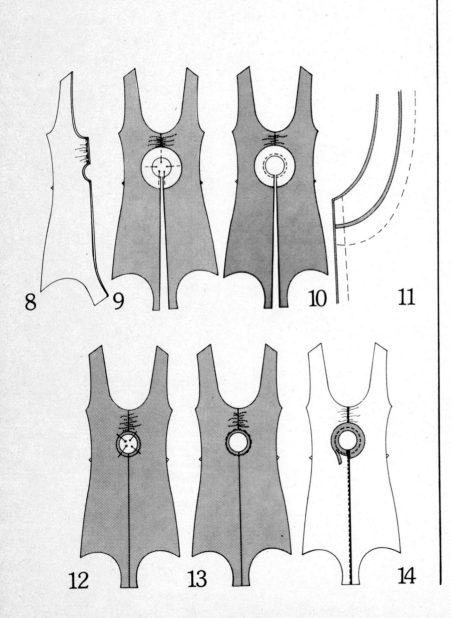

8  9  10  11

12  13  14

thread to gather the center front seam back to the length of the center front seam on the pattern before it was redesigned.

Place the front sections right sides together and sew the center front seam above the circle with a 1/4-inch seam allowance. Start at the lower edge and stretch as you sew. Then, stitch this seam a second time 1/8 inch from the cut edge for reinforcement. (Fig. 8)

For the Chanel-trim finish on your circle opening, cut a strip of fabric that measures 2 inches wide by 10 inches long. This must be cut with the stretch of the fabric going the length of the strip.

Divide the edge of the circle into four equal divisions. Do the same to one edge of the trim. With right sides together, pin the trim to the circle's edge, matching the divisions. (Fig. 9) Stretching the trim evenly as you sew, stitch the trim to the circle with a 1/2-inch seam allowance. (Fig. 10)

Turn the trim toward the opening and place the front sections right sides together. Sew the remaining portion of the center front seam, starting at the lower edge and stitching through the trim. (Fig. 11) Double-stitch this seam up to the seam for the Chanel trim. As you approach the trim, your second line of stitching should be very close to the first stitching line.

Finger-press the center front seam on the trim so that it lies open. Then, fold the trim over the seam allowance for the circle to the wrong side. Pin it carefully so that it is positioned evenly on the outside of the suit. (Fig. 12) Then, stitch-in-the-ditch from the right side around the circle. (Fig. 13) On the inside of the suit, cut away the excess trim close to the stitching line. (Fig. 14)

With a 1/4-inch seam, pin and stitch the center back seam, starting at the lower edge and sewing to the top. Sew a second row of stitching 1/8 inch from the cut edge.

Pin the crotch seam at both edges and at the center. Stitch, using a 5/8-inch seam allowance for this seam. Ease has been allowed on the back section, so it will be necessary for you to stretch the front to match the back. Trim away the back crotch seam allowance to 1/4 inch, leaving the front seam allowance full width. (Fig. 15) Then, fold both seam allowances toward the back of the garment and topstitch through all thicknesses from the right side, 1/2 inch from the seamline. (Fig. 16) Trim close to this stitching line.

Position the lining in the crotch, matching the notches on the lining to the seams of the swimsuit. Pin the lining in place but do not stitch it at this time. (Fig. 17) The crotch lining will be attached when the elastic is sewn at the leg openings.

Place the suit front and back right sides together and sew the side seams from the lower edge to the armscye on each side. Double-stitch as you did the center back and the center front seams. (Fig. 18)

Cut two strips of Stretch & Sew 3/8-inch elastic which measure three-fourths the total measurement of a leg opening. Overlap the ends of the elastic 1/2 inch and stitch them together. (Fig. 19)

Divide the leg openings and the elastic into four equal divisions. Pin the elastic to the inside of the leg openings, matching the divisions. (Fig. 20) On each leg opening, sew along the edge, using a zigzag stitch and taking care to catch the

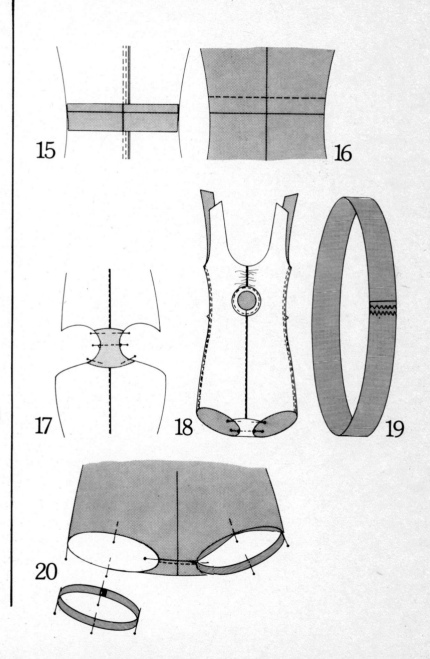

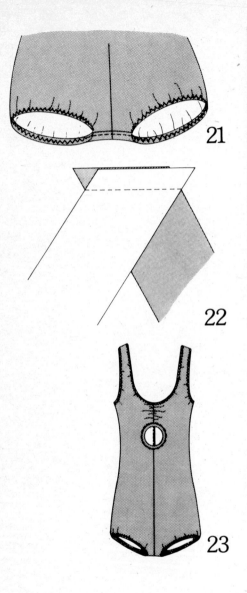

21

22

23

crotch lining in the stitching. Fold the elastic to the inside and zigzag again over the previous stitching line. (Fig. 21)

At this point, you may tack the edges of the lining down at the center front and center back. An easy way to do this is to stitch-in-the-ditch for about 1 inch on either side.

Try the suit on now to check for strap length. A final adjustment in body length can be made at this time by shortening the straps slightly if necessary. After the correct length has been determined, sew the shoulder straps. (Fig. 22) You may double-stitch these seams for extra reinforcement.

Cut a strip of Stretch & Sew 3/8-inch elastic that measures three-fourths the total measurement of the neck edge. Divide the neck edge and the elastic in four equal parts and apply the elastic as you applied the leg elastic.

Stretch & Sew 3/8-inch elastic is also used for the armscye finish. Cut two strips that measure three-fourths the total measurement of an armscye and apply the elastic as you did for the leg openings and the neck edge. (Fig. 23)

Your suit is finished and don't you feel pleased with what you've sewn! For an extra touch, you might make a self-fabric tie to loop through the circle opening and over the top of the suit. Tie it in a bow above the gathers at the center front.

## Variations

### TANK SUIT WITH BRA CUPS

The tank suit is generally seen with the more natural look. However, if you would like to add bra cups to your suit for more shaping and support, you may do so quite easily.

The chart below will help you to determine the correct bra cup size to use for your suit.

| Bra Cup Size | Suit Size |
|---|---|
| 8 | 30 |
| 10 | 32 |
| 12 | 34 |
| 14 | 36 |
| 16 | 38 |
| 18 | 40 |

After you have gathered your front sections and have double-stitched the center front seam above the circle, place the lined bra cups next to the inside of the suit and pin them in place. (Fig. 24) Stretch the fabric to fit smoothly over the cups. Then, stitch close to the edge to secure the bra cup lining to the suit at the neck edge, the armscye, the underarm edge, and at the edge of the circle. Trim the lining even with the edge of the tank suit. Complete the suit according to the instructions given above.

## TANK SUIT WITH SWEETHEART FRONT

On your front pattern piece, draw a line, starting 1-1/4 inches down from the lower edge of the armscye. Curve upward over the bust high point and down as illustrated, ending 1 inch below the center front neck edge. (Fig. 25) Cut on this line. Then, relocate the dart to gathers just as you did for the suit described previously.

On your back pattern piece, draw a line from a point 1-1/4 inches down from the lower edge of the armscye, curving downward to a point 5 inches from the upper edge of the center back. (Fig. 26)

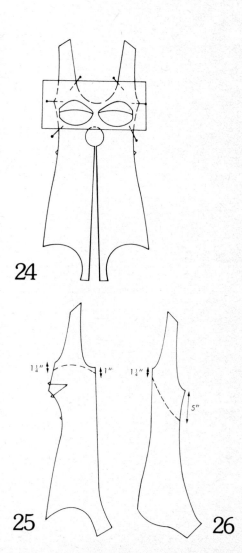

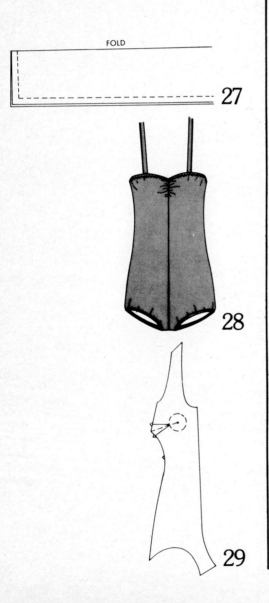

FOLD

27

28

29

Using your adjusted pattern, cut your suit from your fabric. For the neck straps, cut two strips of fabric that measure 2 inches by 18 inches. The greater stretch of the fabric must go crosswise on the straps.

Fold each strap lengthwise with right sides together and stitch across one end and down the long edge with a 1/4-inch seam allowance, stretching hard as you sew. (Fig. 27) Then, turn the straps to the right side. Omitting the steps for the circle cut-out, construct the suit according to the previous instructions up to the application of the elastic at the upper edge.

You will apply 3/8-inch elastic to the top of your suit with a 3:4 ratio. When you position the elastic along the upper edge of the suit, pin the unstitched ends of the straps in place on top of the elastic. The straps should be positioned over the bust high points with the length of the straps extending above the suit. Include the straps in the first stitching of the elastic.

Turn the straps down when you fold the elastic down. Then, turn the straps up and pin them in place to be caught in the second stitching of the elastic. (Fig. 28) When you wear your new swimsuit, simply tie the straps behind your neck!

## PRINCESS LINE TANK SUIT

This princess line variation is flattering for all ages and especially great for competitive swimming. It can easily be made with or without bra cups.

On your front pattern piece, relocate the bustline dart by first extending the center line of the dart 1-1/2 inches. Using the end of this line as a pivot point, draw a circle with a 1-1/2 inch radius. (Fig. 29) Draw the princess line, starting at a point on the armscye about 3 inches above the underarm. Curve the line through the pivot point in the center of your circle and extend it downward, angling toward the side seam slightly at the lower edge as illustrated. (Fig. 30)

Cut the pattern on the princess line and cut the center line of the dart to the pivot point. Close the original underarm dart by bringing the notches at the end of the dart together. (The legs of the dart will not match along their entire length.)

Add a 3/8-inch seam allowance to each edge of the princess line and position notches at the points where the circle around your pivot point crosses the seamlines. (Fig. 31) You are ready to cut your fabric!

The first step in constructing this suit is to sew the princess line seams, matching the notches to make sure you distribute the fullness correctly for the bustline. Finger-press the seam allowances toward the center front of the suit and topstitch them 1/4 inch from the seamline. Then, double-stitch your center front seam and follow the previous instructions for completion of the suit. (Fig. 32)

## Hooded Swim Cover-Up

A swim cover-up is just the thing to go with your new tank suit! While you are coming from the water, a cardigan wrap with a hood will cover you up and protect you from any after-swim chill.

## General Fabric Selection

Many of the fabrics designed for swimsuits are available in a matching fabric — usually nylon

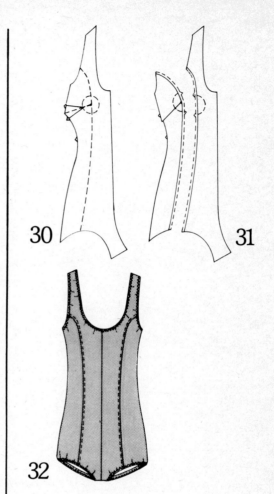

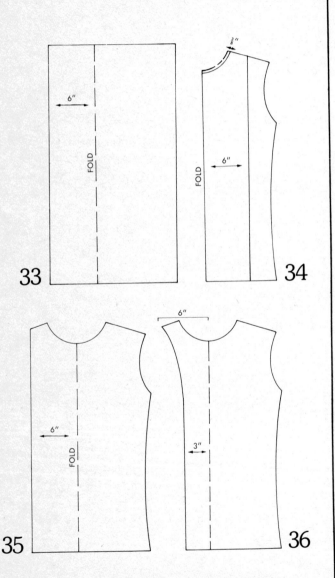

tricot — to provide you with the perfect combination for a splashy-looking outfit.

If you are looking for a warmer fabric that will soak up moisture after a swim, try a terry or a cotton single or double knit. Velour is a wonderful choice for a cover-up when snugness and warmth are important. You may choose one of these fabrics in a solid color to coordinate with your printed swim fabric for a comfortable and attractive cover-up.

## Preparing Your Pattern

Any knit top pattern works fine for this cover-up but I will use the Set-In Sleeve Top and Sweater Pattern 300 for example.

To add a cut-on facing to your pattern, you will need a piece of *Perky* Pattern Paper wide enough to trace half your front pattern piece plus 6 inches. Fold your *Perky* Pattern Paper back 6 inches along one edge. (Fig. 33) On your master pattern, position the fold of the paper on the cardigan line of the front pattern piece. If you are using the children's pattern, which does not indicate the cardigan line, simply place the fold of the pattern material 3/4 inch beyond the center front line on your master pattern.

Trace one size larger than your full bust measurement. Extend the front and back neck edges 3/8 inch. (Fig. 34)

Cut your pattern on the traced lines and unfold the 6-inch extension. (Fig. 35) Starting at the lower edge, trim the facing 3 inches from the fold, tapering out to the full width at the shoulder as illustrated. (Fig. 36) This will create the proper curve for the facing.

For well-finished vents on the side, facings are necessary. Extend the outside lower edge of the front 1 to 1-1/2 inches. Measure 5 to 7 inches up from this point and taper the facing back to the cut edge. (Fig. 37) Make identical extensions on your back pattern piece.

Widen the sleeve pattern by measuring 1 to 1-1/2 inches out on each side at the lower edge and connecting these points at the underarm. (Fig. 38) This will allow you the extra ease which this garment requires.

To make the hood pattern piece for your cover-up, measure from the inside edge of one collar bone, over the top of the head, to the inside edge of the other collar bone. (Fig. 39) Add 2 inches to this measurement. Now, measure from the tip of the nose over the ear to the center of the back of the head as illustrated. (Fig. 40) Using these two measurements, cut a rectangle on your pattern paper. (Fig. 41) This will be your hood pattern.

## Cutting and Sewing Your Garment

Using your adjusted pattern, cut two fronts, one back, two sleeves, and one hood piece from your fabric. You will also need to cut a strip of self-fabric 2 inches wide by the length of the long side of your hood piece. This will provide a Chanel-trim finish for the edge of your hood. Then, cut interfacings for your jacket front facings from *Perky Bond Plus*, trimming 3/8 inch from all edges that will not be placed next to a foldline.

Bond your *Perky Bond Plus* interfacings to the jacket facings. These will provide extra stability under the snap closure or under the buttons and buttonholes.

Sew the shoulder seams right sides together with a 1/4-inch seam allowance.

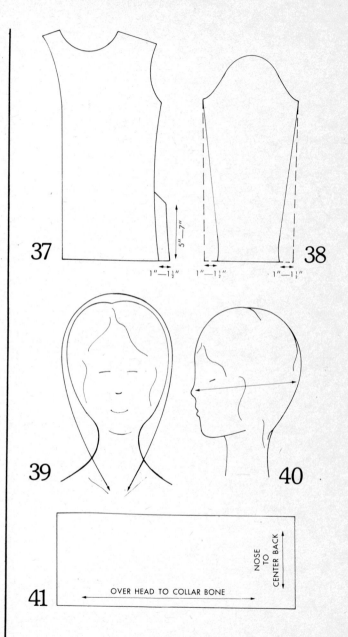

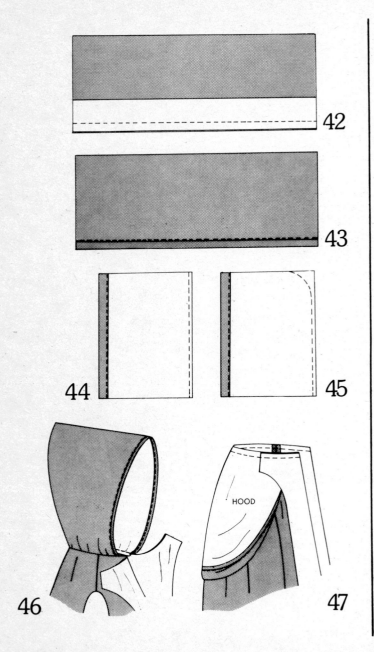

42

43

44      45

46                     47

Divide one long edge of the hood piece and your Chanel trim strip in equal fourths. Position the strip on the hood, right sides together, matching divisions, and stitch with a 1/2-inch seam allowance. (Fig. 42) Press the trim toward the seam allowance. Then, fold the trim to the wrong side and stitch-in-the-ditch from the right side. (Fig. 43) On the wrong side, trim the excess fabric close to the stitching line.

Right sides together, fold the hood section, matching the shorter edges, and stitch the center back seam. (Fig. 44) If you prefer a curved hood that will contour with the shape of your head, start the stitching approximately two-thirds the distance from the front edge on the fold at the top of the hood. Then, curve around to complete the back seam. (Fig. 45)

Sew two rows of gathering stitches around the neck edge of the hood. One row should be 3/4 inch from the edge and the second 1/4 inch from the edge. Right sides together, pin the neck edge of the garment, matching the center backs. On each side the finished edge of the hood should be 1 to 1-1/2 inches back from the facing foldline. Pull the bobbin threads, gathering the hood to fit, and stitch it to the neck edge with a 5/8-inch seam allowance. (Fig. 46)

Turn the facings back at the foldlines, right sides together with the garment front. At this point, the hood will be positioned between the garment front and the facing. On each side, sew over the previous stitching line through all thicknesses. Start at the front fold and overlap stitches where they meet at the center back. (Fig. 47)

Grade the seam allowances along the neck edge. Leave the facing seam allowances full width and leave the hood seam allowance along the back neck edge full width. Turn the facings to their proper position and secure the facings at the shoulder seams. This can be done easily by stitching-in-the-ditch.

With a straight or zigzag stitch, sew the hood seam allowance to the back neck edge of the cover-up from shoulder seam to shoulder seam 3/8 inch from the original seam. (Fig. 48) Trim close to this stitching line.

Right sides together, pin each sleeve to the garment, matching the center of the sleeve to the shoulder seam. The corners at the underarm should also match. As you sew, stretch the armscye to fit the sleeve. (Fig. 49)

Pin the underarm seams right sides together and stitch, starting 1/2 inch below the start of the vent facing and continue to the lower sleeve edge. (Fig. 50) Press the vent facings back in a line continuous with the stitching line. (Fig. 51)

Finish the lower edges of the vent facings by folding them against the garment, right sides together, and stitching at the hemline. (Fig. 52) Trim to the stitching line as illustrated (Fig. 53) and turn the vent facings back to the inside. Finish the lower edges of the center front facings in the same manner.

Hem the lower edge and the sleeve edge by bonding or by machine-stitching. Apply buttons and buttonholes or snaps to the front and you are finished!

# Variations

### REVERSIBLE HOOD

For a reversible hood with an enclosed seam, prepare your hood pattern as previously described

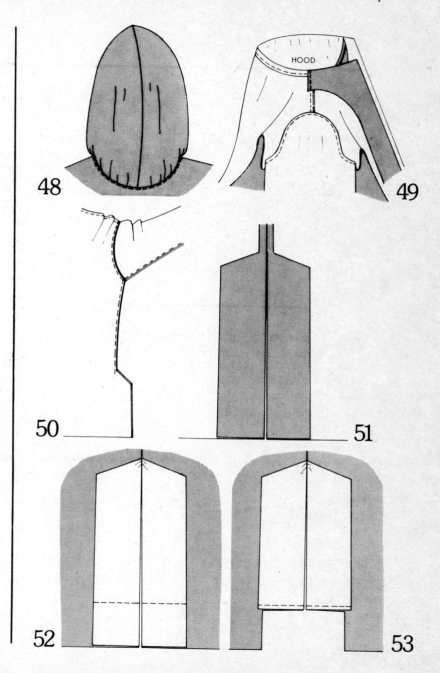

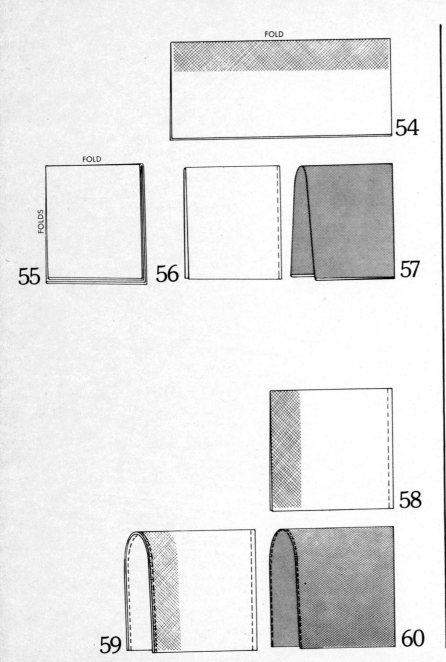

54

55

56

57

58

59

60

and place one long edge on the fold as you cut your fabric.

To provide more body at the front of your hood, cut a strip of *Perky Bond Plus* 4 inches wide by the length of your hood pattern piece. Trim 3/8 inch from the shorter edges. Position this interfacing along the fold of your hood fabric and bond it in place.

Fold your hood fabric in half lengthwise with right sides together. (Fig. 54) Fold it again, matching the shorter edges (Fig. 55), and stitch the center back seam. You will be sewing through four thicknesses. (Fig. 56) Turn the hood to the right side (Fig. 57) and you will have an enclosed seam.

When you sew the hood to the cover-up, position it so that the bonded edge will lie on the underside when the hood is worn.

### REVERSIBLE HOOD WITH CONTRASTING FABRIC

For a reversible hood from contrasting fabric, prepare your hood pattern as previously described and cut one piece from each of your two fabrics.

To provide more body at the front of your hood, cut a strip of *Perky Bond Plus* 4 inches wide by the length of your hood pattern. Trim 3/8 inch from the shorter edges. Bond this interfacing to the front edge of the hood piece which will be on the inside of the hood.

Sew the center back seam of each hood layer. (Fig. 58) Press the seams open and clip the corners at the upper edges. Place the two hood layers right sides together and stitch them along the front edge. (Fig. 59) Press this seam open and turn the hood to the right side. Topstitch 1/4 inch from the front seamline. (Fig. 60) Then, gather the neck edges and apply the hood according to the previous instructions.

## A LONG COVER-UP

You may prefer a longer cover-up than the one described. A-out both the front and back pattern pieces from hip level to the desired length, allowing for the hem. (Fig. 61) The vent on the side seam should be longer on this style than for a shorter cover-up. An average length for the vent is 10 to 12 inches, but it may extend to the thigh.

The garments described in this chapter will start you on your way to a fashionable swim wardrobe. Many of the dart relocations described in Chapter Three of this book are applicable to the tank suit. Simply use your imagination!

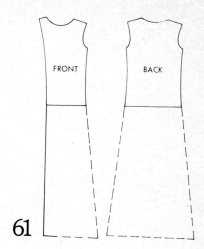

61

# Index

## A

acrylic, 73-74
  jersey, 74
  links, 73-74
alpaca wool, 73
armscye,
  facing, 20-21
  rib trim finished, 81-82
  for sleeveless garment, 20-21, 80
armscye dart, 43-44

## B

banded cardigan jacket (*see* jacket)
banded cardigan vest (*see* vest)
Basic Dress Pattern 1500, 21, 39-53
belt,
  encased elastic, 100-101
  sash, 96
  string tie, 100
belt loops, 31-32
blends, 105
Body Blouse Pattern 790, 39, 89
Boys' Dress Shirt Pattern 930, 89
Boys' Dress Shirt Pattern 935, 89
Boys' Pants Pattern 925, 25
bust high point,
  determining, 40
buttonhole placement, 90, 107

## C

cape,
  with double Chanel trim, 117
cardigan line, 58, 74, 134
cardigan sweater (*see* sweater)
Chanel trim,
  double, on jacket, 108-111, 116-117
  single,
    on hood, 136
    on jacket, 108, 111-115
    on scooped neck with gathers, 47
    on tank swimsuit, 128-129
Children's Raglan Sleeve Top Pattern 862, 57, 73, 125
Children's Set-In Sleeve Top Pattern 861, 3, 73, 125
Children's Straight and Bell-Bottom Pants Pattern 860, 25
coat,
  sleeveless, with self-trim band, 21
collar,
  mandarin, from rib trim, 62-63
  shirtwaist dress, 92
    curved, with trim, 97-98
  square,
    with Chanel trim, 107, 111-113
    with double Chanel trim, 116-117
  turned-down, from rib trim, 63
cover-up (*see* swim cover-up)
crew neck, 7-8